The Tale of Two Bridges and the Battle for the Skies over North Vietnam

USAF Southeast Asia Monograph Series
Volume 1
Monographs 1 and 2

The Tale of Two Bridges

and

The Battle for the
Skies over North Vietnam

Edited by
Major A.J.C. Lavalle

GOVERNMENT REPRINTS PRESS
Washington, D.C.

© Ross & Perry, Inc. 2001 All rights reserved.

No claim to U.S. government work contained throughout this book.

Protected under the Berne Convention. Published 2001

Printed in The United States of America
Ross & Perry, Inc. Publishers
717 Second St., N.E., Suite 200
Washington, D.C. 20002
Telephone (202) 675-8300
Facsimile (801) 459-7535
info@RossPerry.com

SAN 253-8555

Government Reprints Press Edition 2001

Government Reprints Press is an Imprint of Ross & Perry, Inc.

http://www.GPOreprints.com
Library of Congress Control Number: 2001094492

ISBN 1-931641-86-2
Image on cover provided by www.af.mil

⊗ The paper used in this publication meets the requirements for permanence established by the American National Standard for Information Sciences "Permanence of Paper for Printed Library Materials" (ANSI Z39.48-1984).

All rights reserved. No copyrighted part of this publication may be reproduced, stored in a retrieval system, or transmitted, in any form or by any means, electronic, photocopying, recording, or otherwise, without the prior written permission of the publisher.

Foreword

Many documents, articles, and stories have been written about U.S. Air Force operations in Southeast Asia (SEA). However, none have given the critical in-depth coverage commensurate with our level of involvement. This volume, the first in a USAF Southeast Asia Monograph series, is an attempt to document the story of AIRPOWER — and the people behind it — in our nation's longest armed conflict.

For eight years American airmen fought with a multitude of missions, evolving weaponry, ever-changing tactics and maybe most notable — constantly changing constraints. In this volume, authors from the Air War College and Air Command and Staff College who actually fought there have combined for two excellent monographs of the people and weapons in SEA. The authors' breadth of combat experience provides a penetrating account of airpower brought to bear — with all the emotion, frustrations, bravery and confusion of real life.

For the general reader, these stories tell of airpower in human terms and should give some understanding of the spirit, courage, and professionalism of our U.S. airmen. To the student of airpower interested in improving the effectiveness of our Air Force, the monographs make an excellent case study of tactical air doctrine. The entire series is dedicated to ALL who served.

DAVID C. JONES, General, USAF
Chief of Staff
1 January 1976

MONOGRAPH 1

The Tale of Two Bridges

Authors: Colonel Delbert Corum
Lt Colonel Glenn Griffith
Lt Colonel James Jones
Lt Colonel Keith Krause
Lt Colonel Ronald Lord
Lt Colonel Robert Martin
Lt Colonel Malcom Winter
Lt Colonel David Young

Monograph Edited by

Colonel Dewey Waddell
Major Norm Wood

Authors' Acknowledgements

The facilities at Maxwell AFB offer a rich variety of source materials for the study of airpower in Southeast Asia. We are grateful to Mr. Robert B. Lane and his staff at the Air University Library; Lieutenant Colonel Malcolm S. Bounds of the Maxwell CORONA HARVEST office; and Mr. Lloyd H. Cornett, Jr., and his staff at the Albert F. Simpson Historical Research Center.

Dr. Kenneth R. Whiting of the Institute for Professional Development reviewed the manuscripts and provided valuable assistance in the final editing.

Finally, we are indebted to the many Air University personnel who provided support and assistance throughout the project.

—The Authors

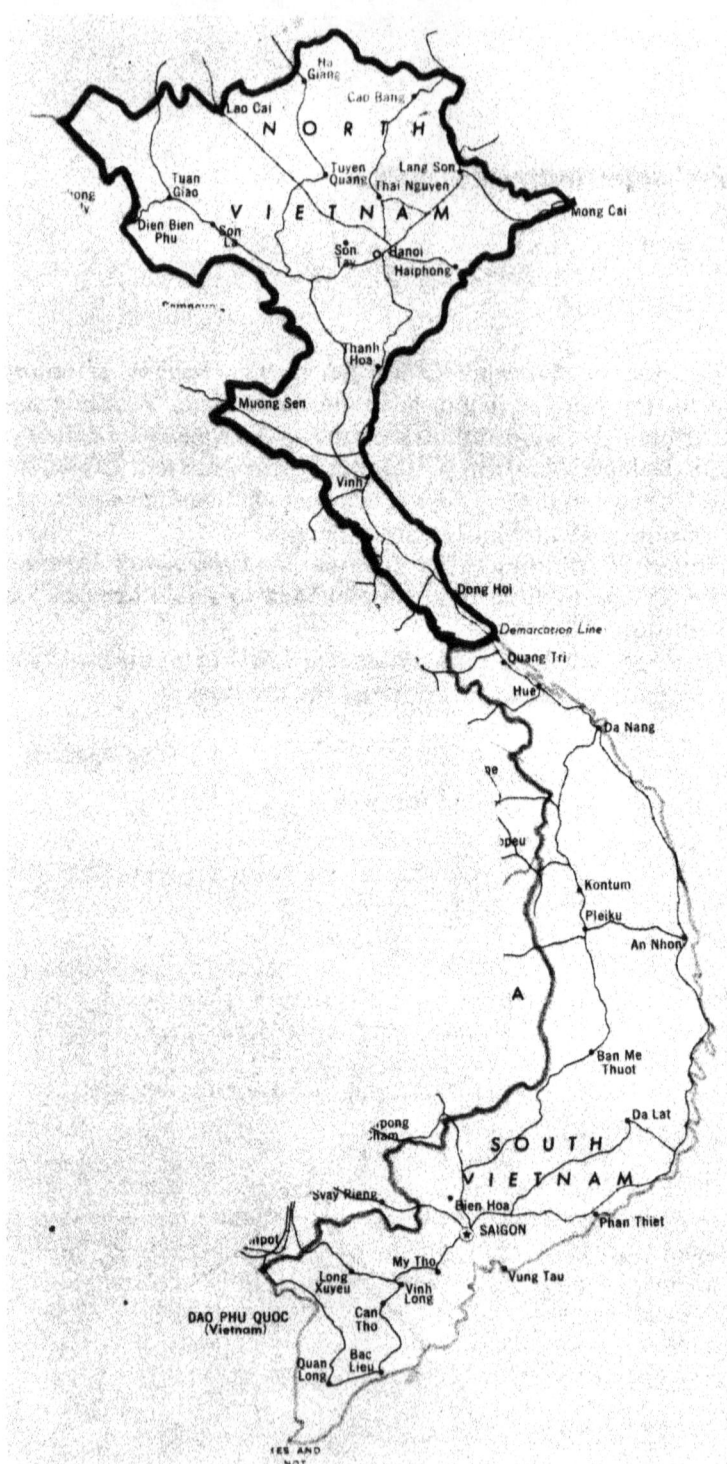

Prologue

This is a story of war. A parable of men and machines, of friend and foe. A drama of moves and countermoves, played out in the skies over North Vietnam and having for its backdrop two bridges — the majestic Paul Doumer and the infamous bridge at Thanh Hoa.

These bridges know well the script of war. The silent contrails high in the blue, the growing dialogue of anti-aircraft fire, the scream of engines, the thunder of bombs, all building to a crescendo. Then subsiding, only to start again in another act on another day. An old play that reopens regularly with new actors — and therein lies our tale.

The curtain went up at the Thanh Hoa Bridge in April 1965, and, as the Vietnam drama unfolded, many new players made their acting debut. Fighters named "Thunderchief" and "Phantom," missiles known as SAMs and SHRIKEs, bombs called "Walleye" and "Smart," and the credits go on. Wild Weasel, Jolly Green, Young Tiger, and MIG Cap — all starred in our long running play as did such names as Carolina Moon and Flaming Dart. Names that flashed brightly across the stage and then were gone.

Actors in a historical play that has now passed into history — leaving us to tell THE TALE OF TWO BRIDGES.

Table of Contents

Prologue	....	ix
Chapter I.	THE SCENE	1
	The Bridges	6
Chapter II.	THE STRIKE AND SUPPORT FORCES	11
	The Strike Aircraft	11
	F-105 Thunderchief	12
	F-4 Phantom II	21
	The Navy Birds	23
	Support Aircraft	23
	Wild Weasel	24
	Aerial Reconnaissance	25
	Combat Air Patrol	26
	Air Refueling: The Tankers	28
Chapter III.	EARLY USAF ATTACKS ON THE THANH HOA BRIDGE	31
Chapter IV.	THREE LONG YEARS	45
	Navy Strikes the Thanh Hoa Bridge	46
	Defense Continues to Improve	50
	Interdiction of the Thanh Hoa-Vinh Rail Line	52
	Project "Carolina Moon"	52
	Strikes Continue Through 1966	56
	The Walleye Glide Bomb	57
	Limited Strikes Through 1967	59
	A Big Strike Ends the First Round	63
	Bombing Halt Comes in Early 1968	63
Chapter V.	THE PAUL DOUMER BRIDGE GOES DOWN .	67
Chapter VI.	BOTH BRIDGES FALL	78
	The Bombing Halt (1968-1972)	78
	Doom of the Dragon	79
	Operation Freedom Dawn	84
	The Dragon Goes Down	85
	Strikes Continue Against the Thanh Hoa Bridge	86
	Doumer's Demise	88

Chapter I. The Scene

The background of the story begins as far back as late 1946 with the French engaged in open warfare with a communist-backed nationalist coalition of guerrillas known as the Viet Minh. Although the struggle was intense, United States attention in those days was focused on Europe. It was not until the triumph of Mao Tse-tung in China that U.S. policy-makers were jolted into extending the ongoing containment of communism to the Far East. Several events followed swiftly—the invasion of South Korea by the North in 1950; U.S. entry into the conflict in Korea, accompanied by massive military assistance; and finally, the defeat of the French by the Viet Minh at Dien Bien Phu on the 7th of May 1954. Thus, U.S. attention was focused on the Far East in almost hypnotic myopia.

The significance of the communist victory in Indochina was that there were now two Vietnamese states—the Democratic Republic of Vietnam (DRV) in the north, and the State of Vietnam in the south (later to become the Republic of Vietnam [RVN]).

To most everyone's surprise, the South Vietnamese began pulling themselves together and were soon receiving considerable American support. A U.S. Military Assistance Advisory Group took over the equipping, training, and advising of the South Vietnamese armed forces which enabled the French military to withdraw completely by early 1956. But, all was not well for the fledgling RVN.

Infiltration of communist guerrillas from the north began to increase and a National Liberation Front was organized in the south to provide an organizational structure for the communists. It appeared to be obvious that Ho Chi Minh and the other leaders in North Vietnam were determined to bring the south under their control.

In November 1963 a coup took place in South Vietnam in which President Ngo Dinh Diem was slain. A parade of inept successors inflicted political chaos on the struggling state and the military situation worsened. In the meantime, U.S. military strength had increased from 685 advisors in 1961 to over 17,00 by 1964.

Officials in Washington felt that more direct military action was needed. The deteriorating situation in South Vietnam persisted and there was a growing conviction that only by carrying the war to

In a major policy decision, Kennedy sent the carrier "Core" to Saigon late in 1961, with helicopters and U.S. advisers.

North Vietnam — to punish and dissuade the North Vietnamese from supporting the insurgency — could the cancer be arrested.

The idea of putting direct pressure on North Vietnam was well received by President Johnson. Early in 1964 the President directed that contingency plans be drawn up for air strikes and overt military pressure against North Vietnam! The stage had been set and it would appear that the curtain was about to go up. The Joint Chiefs of Staff (JCS) directed the Commander of all U.S. forces in the Pacific theater (CINCPAC) to select appropriate targets.

In the aftermath of the Diem coup, Gen Duong Van Minh announces the formation of ruling junta. At rear, second from right, is Nguyen Van Theiu, later to become President.

Gen Earle Wheeler briefing the President at the White House. At left is Gen John McConnell, at rear Gen Harold Johnson.

The plan which was drawn up, and approved by the JCS on April 17, 1964, contained a list of 94 of the most important targets in North Vietnam. CINCPAC felt that destruction of these targets was essential if an air campaign against North Vietnam was to be effective. The twelfth target on the list was the Paul Doumer Rail and Highway Bridge located on the outskirts of Hanoi; the fourteenth was the Thanh Hoa Rail and Highway Bridge located just north of the city of Thanh Hoa, seventy miles south of Hanoi. Both of these bridges were key links in the North Vietnamese transportation system, and they were destined to become two of the most famous — or infamous — targets in North Vietnam.

Little did one realize that the lights were dimming, the orchestra was in place, and all that remained was the hush of anticipation that precedes the conductor. . . .

The baton was lifted; on the 2nd and 4th of August, North Vietnamese patrol boats attacked the U.S. destroyers in the Gulf of Tonkin. Act I began. Reprisal attacks were launched by the Navy from aircraft carriers against the enemy torpedo boats and their fuel storage facilities. Two days later both Houses of Congress passed a near-unanimous "Tonkin Gulf Resolution" which authorized the President to use armed force in the area.

For the next several months, isolated reprisal attacks were made against North Vietnam just north of the demilitarized zone (DMZ). It was not until February 13, 1965, that President Johnson made the decision to inaugurate a sustained, but in many ways limited, air campaign against North Vietnam. This program bore the code name "Rolling Thunder." Truly the thundering percussion would appear to roll on and on and on in the next few years.

The initial series of Rolling Thunder air strikes were both political and psychological in nature. Target selection, forces, munitions used, and even timing of the strikes were decided in Washington. Targets struck were barracks, radar sites, ammunition depots, and military vehicles — all in the southernmost part of North Vietnam.

Meanwhile, the JCS stressed the need to interdict the North Vietnamese lines of communication (LOC) if there were to be any reduction of the flow of men and material into South Vietnam. The destruction of the southern portion of the railway system became the highest priority. Military planners pointed out that south of the 20th parallel there existed 115 miles of useable rail line; the vulnerable points on this line were five large bridges and the rail yard at Vinh. The JCS recommended that this rail system be attacked and destroyed immediately. Since the DRV could reasonably be expected to take both passive and active defensive measures, the entire southern portion of the rail system should be hit in a single effort. The Dang Phuong Rail and Highway Bridge and the Thanh Hoa bridge should be the first targets attacked in order to trap the maximum quantity of rolling stock south of the 20th parallel where it could then be destroyed.

The Secretary of Defense accepted the JCS' recommendation. The Joint Chiefs, and Air Force Chief of Staff General McConnell in particular, believed that the most successful interdiction strategy would be one of short duration and broad scope. General McConnell argued for a 28-day air campaign in which all of the 94 targets on the JCS list would be destroyed, including those around Hanoi.

On March 27, 1965, the JCS submitted a four-phase program to Secretary McNamara which incorporated some, but not all, of General McConnell's views. This was to be a twelve-week program intended to isolate North Vietnam from all external sources of resupply, and then to destroy her internal military and industrial capacity.

Phase 1 (three weeks) aimed at interdicting all LOCs south of the 20th parallel, beginning with an attack on the Thanh Hoa Rail and Highway Bridge.

Phase 2 (six weeks) called for severing all rail and highway links with China, including the destruction of the Paul Doumer Rail and Highway Bridge.

Phase 3 (two weeks) visualized air attacks against all port facilities, the mining of seaward approaches during the ninth week, and the destruction of ammunition and supply dumps during the tenth week.

Phase 4 (two weeks) was the wind-up phase, devoted to restriking

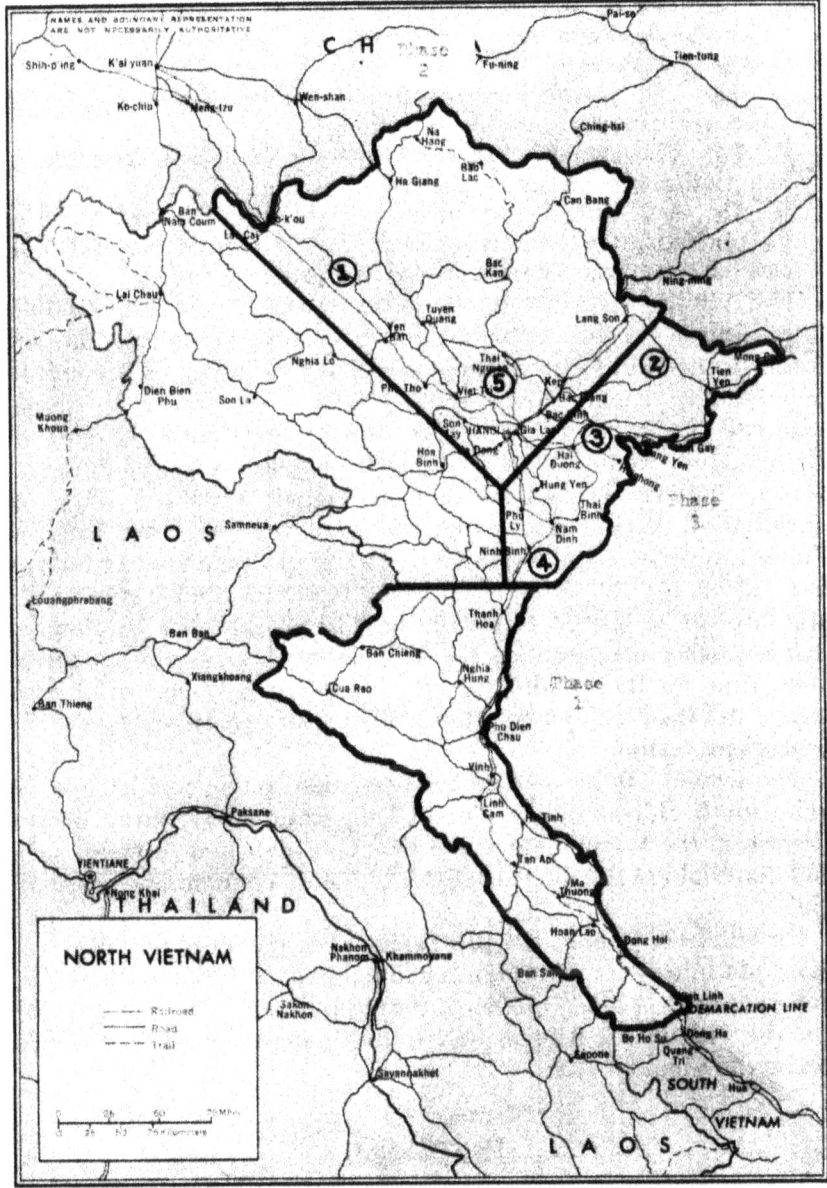

all the previous targets as necessary, as well as attacks on industrial targets that were outside populated areas.

The initial targets in this four-phase, twelve-week air campaign were to be the key bridges in the North Vietnamese railroad system which comprised five major lines, as follows:

#1: The 140-mile northwest rail line connecting Hanoi with the south-central Chinese rail system;

#2: The 82-mile northeast rail line providing an important rail link between the southeastern Chinese supply concentrations and Hanoi;

#3: The 40-mile eastern rail link between Hanoi and North Vietnam's major port city, Haiphong;

#4: The 165-mile southern rail line, extending from Hanoi south through Thanh Hoa and Vinh to the DMZ; and

#5: A 45-mile stretch of track from a mining area north of Thai Nguyen to the northeast rail line ten miles north of Hanoi, which served the Thai Nguyen iron and steel complex.

The Achilles' Heel of this rail system lay on the outskirts of Hanoi where four of the five major rail lines came together to cross the Red River on the Paul Doumer Railroad/Highway Bridge. The destruction of this bridge would sever Hanoi from southwest China, southeast China and the major North Vietnamese seaport at Haiphong. It would also interdict National Route 1, the most important highway leading north from Hanoi. With this route interdicted all truck traffic would have to be rerouted from National Route 1 to routes 2 and 3 located northwest of Hanoi and served by a ferry across the Red River. Haiphong to Hanoi road traffic would also have to be ferried across the Red River. The JCS emphasized that any delay in authorizing the destruction of this key bridge would allow time for the building of an extensive by-pass system of river ferries and the development of an effective air defense system for the bridge's protection.

The second bridge marked for early destruction was located 70 miles south of Hanoi, the Thanh Hoa Railroad/Highway Bridge (known to the Vietnamese as the Dragon's Jaw) that funneled men and material toward the battlefields in South Vietnam and southern Laos.

For whatever reason, the JCS twelve-week bombing program was never put into effect. However, a campaign against the southern rail line was begun in March 1965. In the ensuing years the Paul Doumer and the Thanh Hoa Bridges were to be among the most famous targets in the Vietnam War.

The Bridges

The 1,300 mile railway system was conceived by the Governor General of French Indochina, Paul Doumer, and built between 1896 and 1902. The system was never used effectively by the French. For the North Vietnamese in the 1960's, however those 1,300 miles of rail line were a major factor in the movement of military supplies from China and Haiphong into Hanoi and thence south to the battlefields. All the supplies coming into Hanoi by rail passed over the Paul Doumer Bridge, while those moving southward crossed the Thanh

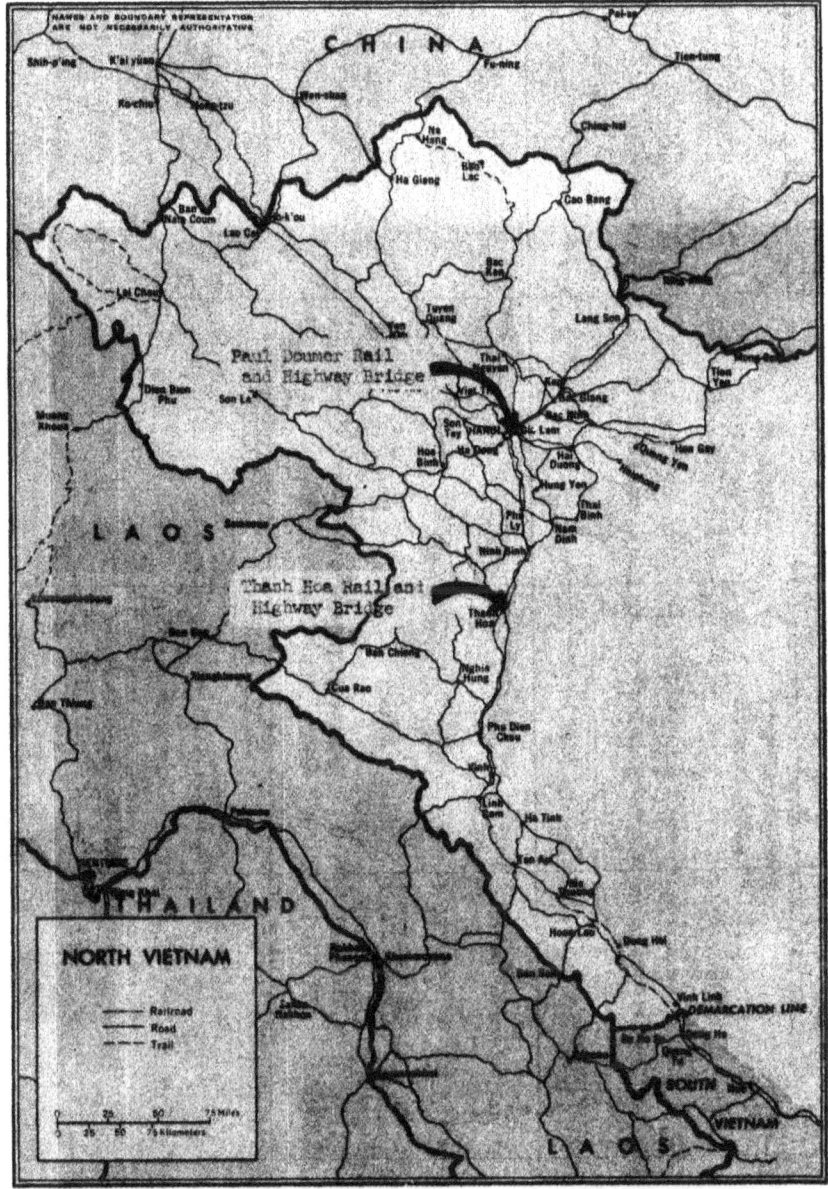

Hoa Bridge. Both bridges also served as funnels for truck and other vehicle convoys.

The Paul Doumer Bridge, on the outskirts of Hanoi, originally served as the rail entry to Hanoi for both the east (Haiphong) and the west (Lao Cai) lines. Later, it also serviced feeder lines from Kep, Thai Nguyen, and Dong Dang to the north. The nineteen-span steel bridge crosses the Red River in an area of low, flat flood plains. With the exceptions of Hanoi to the west and south, and the in-

The Paul Doumer Bridge.

dustrial area near the Gia Lam airport to the east, the bridge is set in the midst of compact villages and small towns scattered throughout the rice paddies.

The bridge—5,532 feet in length and 38 feet wide—was the longest in North Vietnam, with a one-meter gauge railway track in the center and a ten-foot highway on each side. Resting on eighteen massive concrete piers, there were ten thru-thrust spans (eight of 350 feet and two of 250 feet) and nine cantilever spans (each 246 feet). Since the approach viaducts measured 2,935 feet, the total length of the structure was 8,467. Although these figures are impressive in their own right, no one realized just how profound they were until the attacks began.

The Thanh Hoa Bridge, which spans the Song Ma River, is located three miles north of the town of Thanh Hoa, the capital of Annam Province. It is a replacement for the original French-built bridge which was destroyed by the Viet Minh in 1945—they simply loaded two locomotives with explosives and ran them together in the middle of the bridge.

In 1957, the North Vietnamese, with the assistance of Chinese technicians, undertook the task of again spanning the swift-flowing Song Ma. Using construction methods that were crude by western standards, the project moved along ponderously until 1961 when the regime in Hanoi, needing the bridge to facilitate the movement of supplies to the insurgents in the south, put on the pressure. By working 24-hours a day, the builders completed the bridge in 1964, and Ho Chi Minh himself presided at the dedication.

The new bridge at Thanh Hoa was called the Ham Rung (or Dragon's Jaw) by the Vietnamese. It was 540 feet long, 56 feet wide, and about 50 feet above the river. The Dragon's Jaw had two steel thru-truss spans which rested in the center on a massive reinforced concrete pier, 16 feet in diameter, and on concrete abutments at the other ends. Hills on both sides of the river provided solid bracing for the structure. Between 1965 and 1972, eight concrete piers were added near the approaches to give additional resistance to bomb damage. A one-meter gauge single railway track ran down the 12-foot wide center and 22-foot wide concrete highways were cantilevered on each side. This giant would prove to be one of the single most challenging targets for U.S. air power.

Thus in early 1965, as President Johnson and his top advisors pondered the JCS plan to pressure Hanoi into a cessation, or at least an attenuation, of its support for the insurgency in South Vietnam, the Paul Doumer and Thanh Hoa Bridges stood out as vital links in the enemy's transportation system. The American forces destined to strike at the North Vietnamese logistical system were gathering at bases throughout South Vietnam and Thailand. The long and arduous air war against the bridges was about to begin.

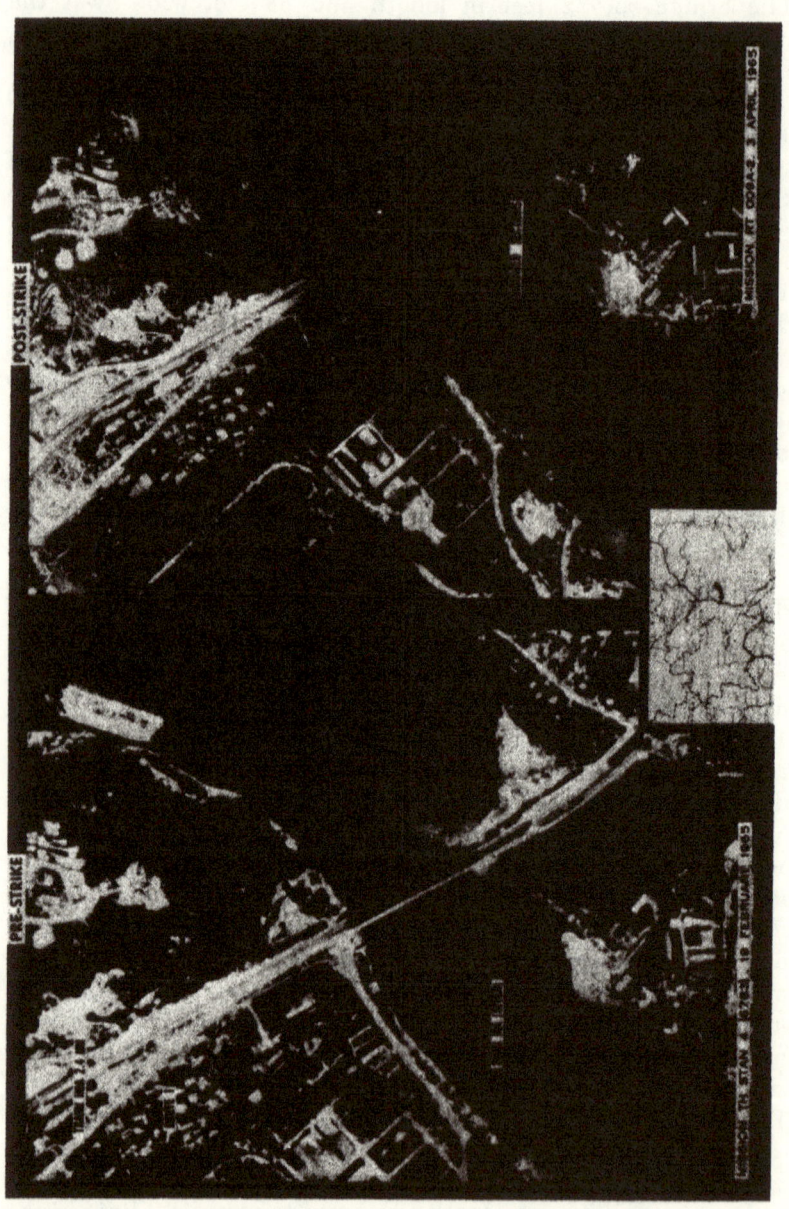

The Thanh Hoa Bridge.

Chapter II. The Strike and Support Forces

As will become evident when the attacks on the Paul Doumer and Thanh Hoa Bridges are described in detail, modern airpower involves a very close relationship between men and machines, between the airmen and their vehicles and weapons systems. In addition, the whole effort must be backed up by adequate ground support. Thus it would seem fitting at this point to describe the considerable array of aircraft, weapons systems, and sophisticated electronic gadgetry used to "bust the bridges." This is not the description of a static situation; between 1965 and 1972 a bitter contest evolved between Hanoi's Soviet-supplied defensive weapons and the US offensive means. Russian MIGs, surface-to-air missiles (SAMs), and better radar elicited more sophisticated US offensive weapons and new evasive tactics. The high explosive (HE) bomb, a seeming constant in the ever changing offensive-defensive counterpoint, made a quantum jump with the advent of the guided bomb.

The Strike Aircraft

Throughout the long and often frustrating Vietnam war, tactical aircraft were called upon to carry the primary strike burden against highly defended targets in North Vietnam. Many of the combat missions could be considered as strategic bombardment rather than as tactical interdiction because of the type of targets attacked, the desired long range effects, and the aerial refueling required for deep penetration. However, the extremely hostile environment in and around the important North Vietnamese targets plus political reservations about committing strategic bombers made the use of fighters a necessity. Tactical fighters—with their superior speed, maneuverability and weapons delivery flexibility—proved to be well suited for this critical role.

The two primary strike aircraft used by the USAF against targets in North Vietnam were the F-105 "Thunderchief" and the F-4 "Phantom." These aircraft, and US Navy tactical fighters, will be long remembered for the outstanding contributions they made to the "out-country[1]" war in SEA and, in particular, as the Paul Doumer and Thanh Hoa "bridge busters."

F-105 Thunderchief

The Thunderchief first entered the Air Force tactical inventory in 1959. Designed and built by Republic for high speed, low-level delivery of weapons, the F-105 was a technologically superior fighter-bomber aircraft. The design model progressed from the YF-105A[2] in 1955 through the F-model in 1962. The significant technologies were the "coke bottle" design which reduced airplane drag at supersonic speeds, and a highly sophisticated, precision navigation and weapon-delivery system. The F-model offered the two-seat configuration which was to play a signal role in the "Wild Weasel" SAM and radar suppression mission during the Vietnam war.

For the Thunderchief the air war in North Vietnam began on 2 March 1965, when F-105s took part in a strike against the Xom Bong ammunition storage area near the DMZ. This and other early missions were flown by aircrews and aircraft placed on temporary duty (TDY) in Thailand from other bases in the Pacific. At that time, PACAF possessed three kinds of aircraft that could be used in a tactical strike role—the F-105, F-100 and B-57. Largest in number were the F-105s with approximately 150 aircraft available.

As the tempo of the war increased, additional F-100 and F-105 squadrons were deployed to SEA from bases in the US. It was soon obvious that the F-105 was superior to the F-100 for the strike role against targets in North Vietnam, especially those in the country's highly defended interior. With its size and range, the F-105 could carry twice the bomb load, farther and faster than the F-100. By early 1966, two wings of F-105s were permanently stationed in Thailand—the 355 Tactical Fighter Wing (TFW) at Takhli and the 388 TFW at Korat. During the Rolling Thunder Campaign, 1965-1968, the F-105s performed more than 75 per cent of all strike missions against North Vietnam. Throughout the campaign, the Thunderchiefs were the primary USAF weapons delivery system employed against both the Thanh Hoa and Paul Doumer Bridges. The F-105 Thunderchief was one of the largest and heaviest single seat fighter aircraft in the world (maximum take off weight over 50,000 pounds). This immense size prompted pilots to tag the F-105 with some of the most unflattering nicknames ever given to a fighter

---

[1]"Out-country" was the popular term for the air war against North Vietnam. "In-country referred to the conflict within South Vietnam itself.

[2]"Y" prefix denotes prototype and "A" suffix denotes first model design; subsequent models are identified alphabetically.

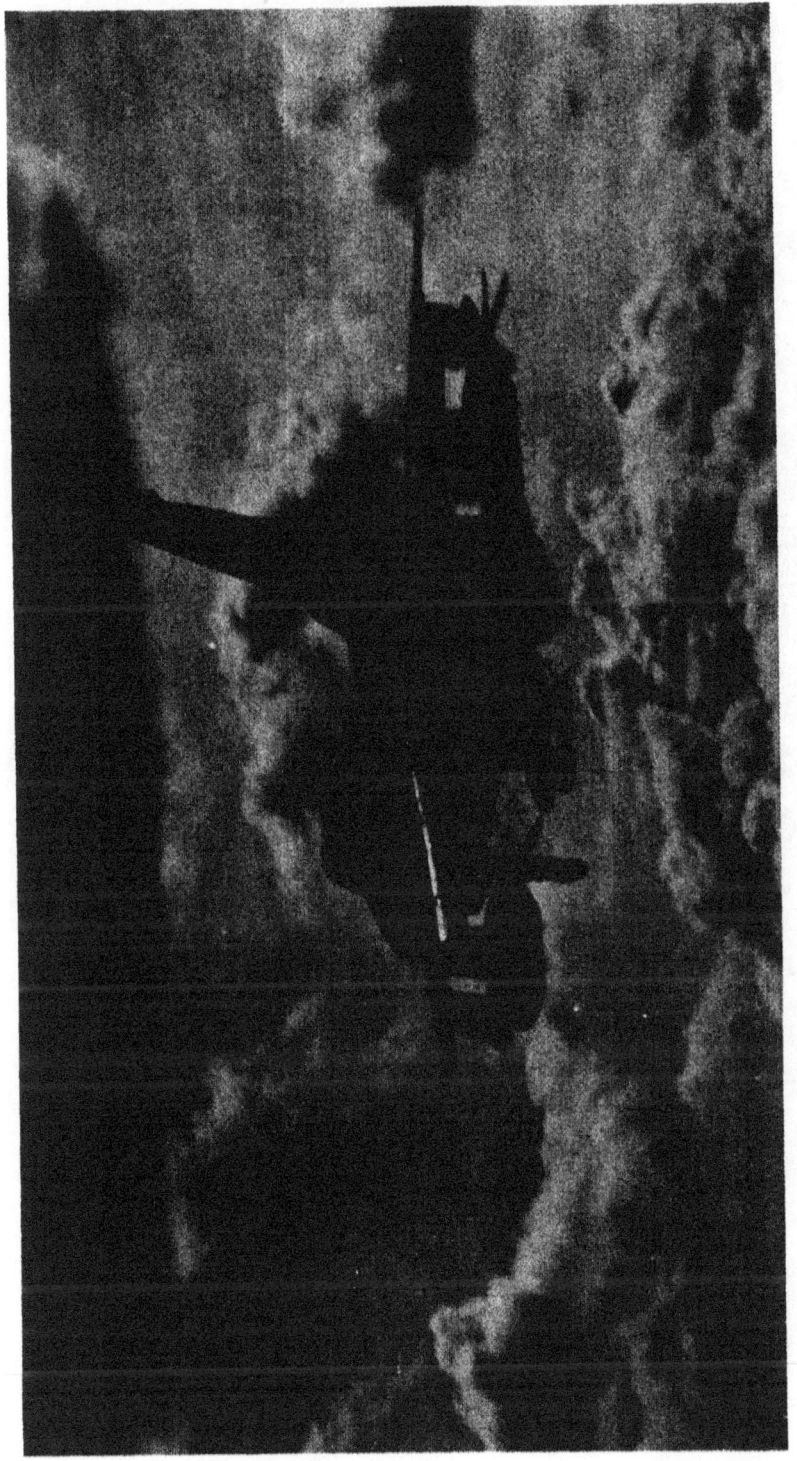

An F-105D, with after-burner glowing, taking off from Korat Air Base, Thailand, on a bombing mission.

The day-in, day-out flying of the F-105s over North Vietnam meant around-the-clock maintenance. Photo shows airmen grooming an F-105D for an early morning mission.

plane. The most famous and one that is synonymous with the F-105 today is simply the "Thud," a term first used sarcastically and, later, with affection. Others acquiring some degree of notoriety were "Lead sled," "Ultra-Hog," and "Squash bomber." Even some of the names painted on its fuselage, such as "25 Ton Canary" and "Iron Butterfly," were brilliantly descriptive. Obviously these names were

An F-105D enroute to a target deep in North Vietnam being refueled by a KC-135 tanker.

used in jest, as few aircraft will ever command the admiration, affection and respect that the F-105 earned from its pilots and ground crewmen.

The F-105 could carry an awesome array of armaments and other stores on five external stations, including fuel tanks, conventional bombs, rockets, missiles, and tactical nuclear weapons. To complement the external armament, a 20mm "Vulcan" cannon was mounted inside the aircraft to provide greater air-to-air and air-to-ground capabilities. This fantastic gun operated on the rotating barrel principle and could fire 6,000 rounds per minute.

The F-105, however, did have some limitations which tested the mettle of both pilots and ground crews. Fully loaded, it required an uncomfortably long takeoff roll. Hydraulic lines of the dual flight control system running side-by-side, made it possible for enemy fire to knock out both systems at once and render the aircraft uncontrollable. To alleviate this, an emergency system was installed while the aircraft were in Thailand, which enabled the pilot to get back over friendly territory for bail out. The 105's relatively small wing area (385 square feet and 45-degree sweep) created high wing loading during maneuvers. Old-time fighter pilots mumbled about the Thunderchief's inability to turn effectively during air-to-air engagements. They soon learned to depend instead upon the F-105's great speed to outrun MIGs which attacked while inbound to target and to use that speed to chase MIGs after bomb delivery.

The "Thud's" unbelievable toughness endeared it to the hearts of the pilots who flew it against heavily defended targets. Because of its ability to absorb punishment, many a Thunderchief returned to a friendly base despite gaping holes in wing, stabilizer, or fuselage. The experience of Major William McCelland testifies vividly to the "Thud's" ruggedness. On 28 June 1966, Major McClelland attacked a heavily traveled highway bridge in North Vietnam and as he pulled off on his dive bomb pass, an 85mm shell hit the 450-gallon fuel tank beneath the right wing. The shell exploded in the pylon and continued laterally along and through the wing tearing out everything for about four feet. In spite of the great drag generated by the enormous hole and protruding wing sections, Major McClelland was able to "nurse" his Thud some 500 miles to his home base and made a successful landing. Another F-105 was hit by an air-to-air missile which lodged in the aft section of the aircraft. Although the entire rear portion of the Thunderchief was heavily damaged, the aircraft landed safely with its unique cargo.

By 1972 most of the "Thuds" had been replaced by the F-4 Phantoms. Nevertheless, some still remained to see action in a SAM killer and flak suppression role. General William Momyer, former commander of the Seventh Air Force, paid special tribute to the F-105's overall contribution to the war in Vietnam. He pointed out that its

An F-105D landing at Korat AB, Thailand, after a successful bombing mission.

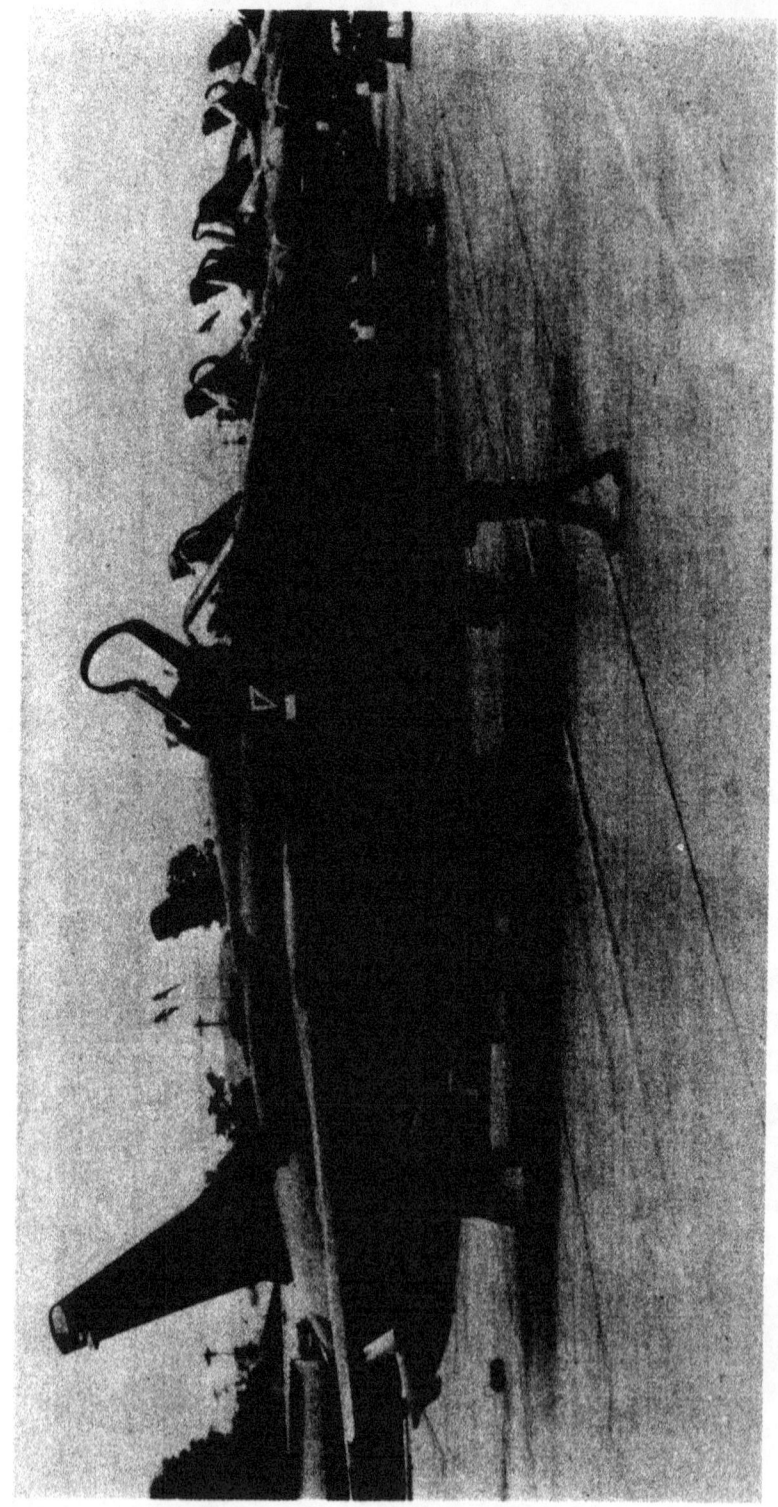
An F–105D loaded with 750-lb bombs starting to taxi for take-off on a bombing mission.

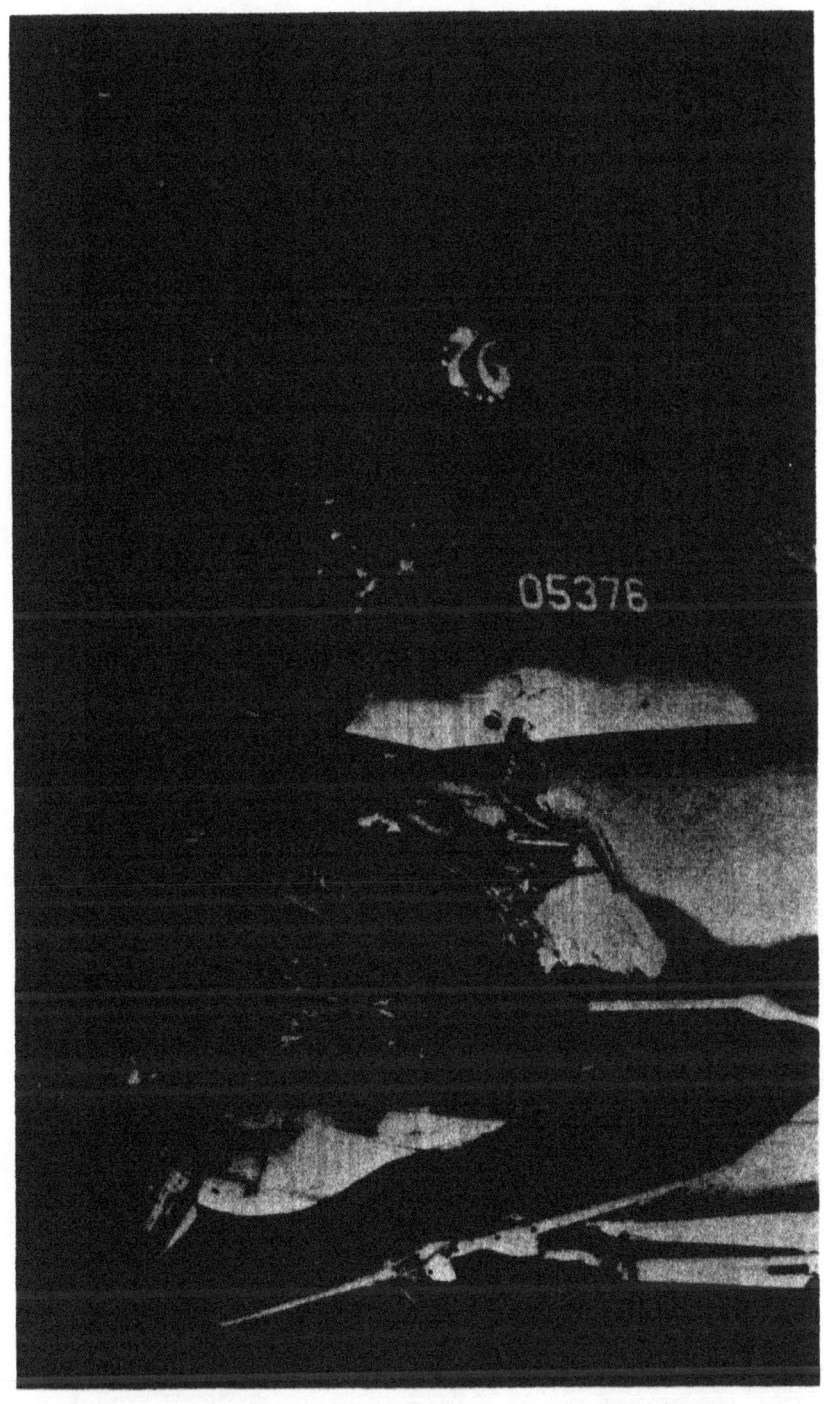

An F-105 after being hit by an air-to-air missile. Booster is visible imbedded in aircraft tail section.

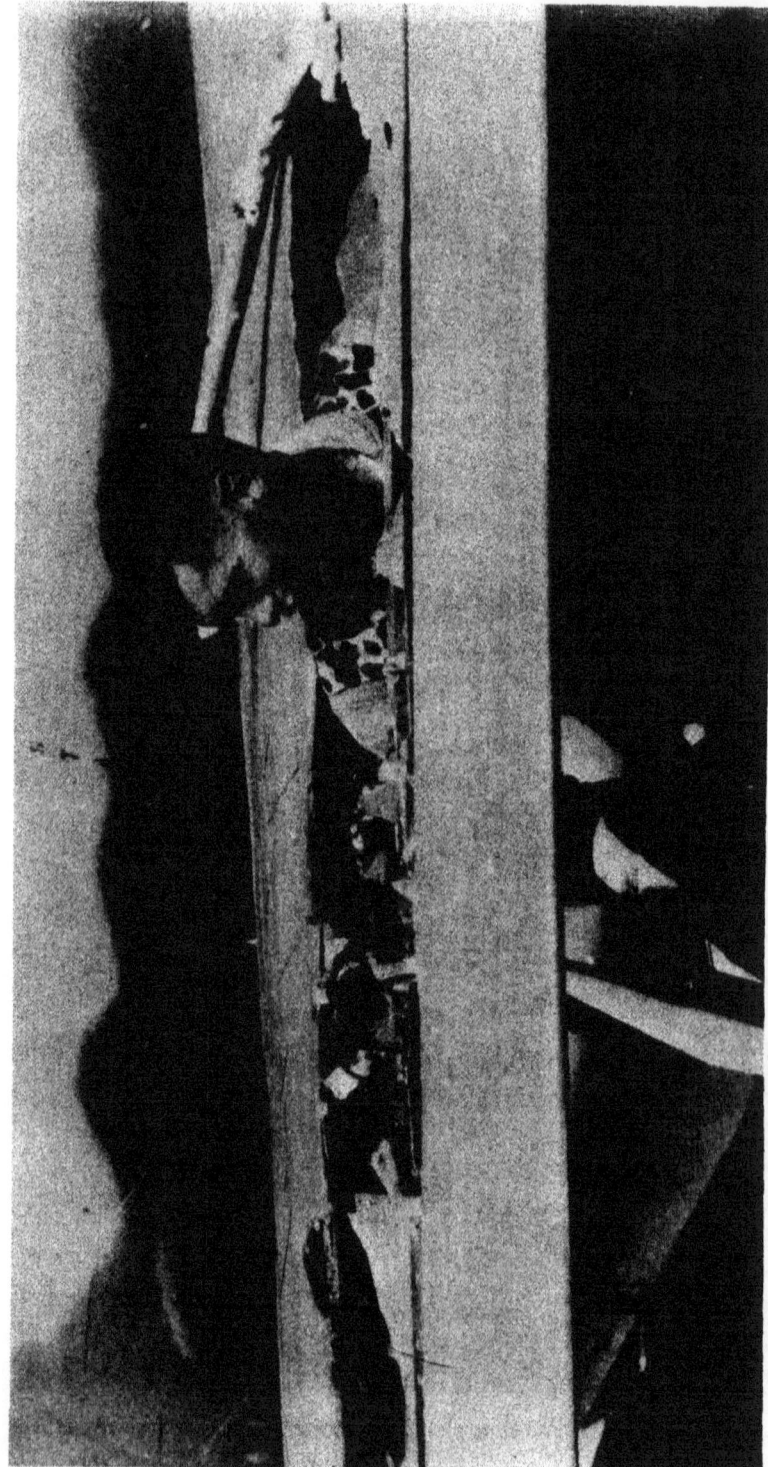

Major McClelland stands in the hole left by an 85mm shell which hit the wing of his F-105.

outstanding speed and ruggedness helped the USAF carry the war to the heart of the enemy. In his opinion, its speed at low altitudes and its high performance made it the finest aircraft in the war.

F-4 Phantom II

The other USAF fighter to carry the war into North Vietnam was the McDonnel-Douglas F-4 Phantom, which proved to be the most versatile combat aircraft employed during the Southeast Asia conflict. It could perform the diversified roles of air superiority, close air support, interdiction, air defense and long range bombardment with devastating effectiveness. With this flexibility, the Phantom was used for practically every purpose in SEA—from delivering weapons with the timely and pin-point accuracy required to support ground troops in the south to performing the critical and demanding strike role in the north. It was superb also in the specialized roles of reconnaissance, Wild Weasel, and MIG CAP. Although the Phantom got most of its publicity as a "MIG killer," it was its excellent bombing capability, especially its many trips "to the bridges," that is pertinent to our story.

A camouflage-painted F-4C in flight over North Vietnam.

The F-4, initially an all-weather, high-altitude, two-place interceptor used by the Navy for fleet defense, made its maiden flight in May 1958. With two powerful engines, it easily reaches speeds over Mach 2, and has a maximum altitude near 60,000 feet.

Because of its bent-up wing tips and drooping horizontal tail (both for aerodynamic stability), the F-4 has been described as "brutishly ugly in appearance." But the aircrews who flew the Phantom in combat, shot down MIGs, bombed heavily defended targets, and made it home in severely crippled machines, thought it a beautiful bird.

The F-4 became the first jet fighter fathered by the Navy to go into the Air Force inventory when it was acquired by the Tactical Air Command in 1962. A long-range inertial navigation system, air-to-ground missile capability, and flight controls in the rear cockpit where the main changes required in the Air Force model, the F-4C.

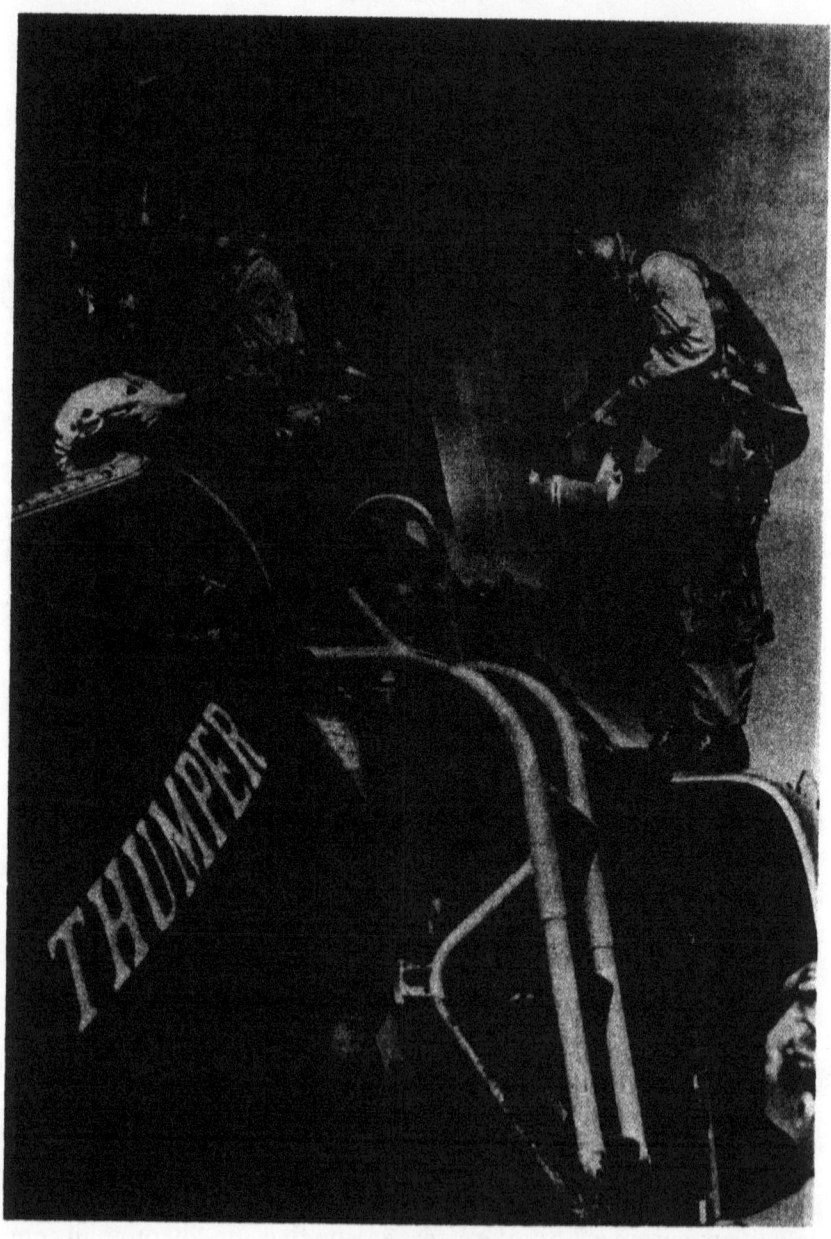

USAF Lt Col Gene Levy (left) and Lt Bob Hand climb into the cockpit of their F-4 for a combat mission.

This Phantom could carry 8 tons of munitions, or other combinations of fuel tanks and armaments—a most impressive strike capability.

The F-4D, which followed, incorporated an improved accuracy in air-to-ground delivery and an air-to-air gunnery capability. It was not until late 1967, however, that the F-4E with its internal cannon came into the inventory, too late for the Rolling Thunder operations, but used extensively in the Linebacker campaign of 1972.

The first Phantoms arrived in SEA in April 1965 and by the end of 1966 there were three F-4 wings in the area. Initially employed to augment the F-105s in Rolling Thunder, the Phantom became the USAF's primary strike aircraft in the 1972 Linebacker campaign.

As with any aircraft, the F-4 had some limitations. Like the F-105, the F-4 hydraulic systems were vulnerable to ground fire and could result in loss of flight controls if hit. Cockpit visibility was restricted due to the structure of the aircraft causing a blind spot in the rear. The engines produced a heavy black smoke, which helped both enemy MIG pilots and ground gunners to see, identify, and track the F-4. The positive features—two engine reliability, a two-man crew, high power-to-weight ratio, and moderate wing loading—more than made up for any deficiencies.

The Navy Birds

The US Navy played the major role in the war on the Thanh Hoa Bridge and a lesser one against the Paul Doumer Bridge, flying their sorties from aircraft carriers in the Gulf of Tonkin. Six different aircraft were used in the Navy's bridge-busting operations: the A-3, A-4, A-6, A-7, F-4, and F-8. The Navy's workhorse against the bridges was the A-4 Skyhawk, a single-engine, single-seat attack aircraft. The A-4 flew some 208 sorties against the Thanh Hoa Bridge, more than three times that of any other Navy aircraft. The A-6 Intruder, a twin-engine, two-phase attack bomber, was the Navy's only all-weather attack plane and was kept busy. The F-4B Phantom II, basically the same as the Air Force F-4, was used extensively in an attack role. The A-3 Skywarrior, a twin-engine attack bomber saw little action against the bridges, going at Thanh Hoa only twice. The F-8 Crusader, a single-engine, single-seat all-weather interceptor, saw action against Thanh Hoa only nine times—its main role was that of a MIG killer. Finally, the A-7 Corsair II, designed as the replacement for the A-4, was introduced in the theatre in late 1967 and did not get into bridge-busting until 1972.

Support Aircraft

The complex of SAMs and radar-directed anti-aircraft artillery (AAA) in North Vietnam evolved from a fairly primitive capability in 1965 to the most concentrated and deadly air defense in history by 1972. Since the heaviest concentrations of SAMs and AAA were around key areas, both the Paul Doumer and Thanh Hoa Bridges got very generous allotments. Again, there was a technological escalation on both sides; as the enemy's air defense system evolved quantitatively and qualitatively, the US offensive capabilities grew ever more sophisticated. The strike pilots, flying against the most heavily defended areas in the history of aerial warfare, needed lots of help in accomplishing their missions.

This help came from supporting aircraft and crews that accomplished those missions so essential in getting strike pilots to the target and home again. Reconnaissance crews to find and photograph targets; tankers to supply fuel; the MIG CAP to parry enemy interceptor aircraft; and search and rescue forces to pick up downed airmen — all are vitally important and well established supporting players in the scenario of an air battle. Albeit, these better known participants were overshadowed in Southeast Asia by a new entry in the field of combat support — the Wild Weasel.

Wild Weasel

This new weapons system combined a pilot and an electronic warfare officer (EWO) in a tactical fighter aircraft, a combination descriptively called "Weasel" because its job was to ferret out and suppress or destroy the enemy's SAM, AAA, and AW (automatic weapons) installations.

The strike pilots relied heavily on the Wild Weasels throughout the Vietnam war, especially in heavily defended areas such as those around the Paul Doumer and Thanh Hoa Bridges. The "Weasels" took on the SAMs while the strike force went for the targets. The courage of the Wild Weasel provides us an excellent example of supporting forces that are invaluable in air operations.

Obviously, the Wild Weasel mission was not an enviable one, and American flying men often say that the call of the Wild Weasel is, "How in the hell did I get into this business?" But that jibe is only a respectful salute from fellow aviators who saw the Weasels write a glowing chapter of heroism in the SAM filled skies of North Vietnam while adding a new dimension to the art of tactical air warfare.

Clear proof of the high risk factor associated with the Wild Weasel I tactics came early, 20 December 1965, when Captains John Pitchford and Bob Trier became the first Wild Weasel crew shot down. On this occasion, Captain Pitchford, flying a specially-fitted F-100F, was guiding four F-105s inland. Just north of Haiphong, the rattlesnake sound of a "Fan Song" radar was detected. As the F-100F crew stalked the quarry, the flak became extremely heavy and a 37 mm shell exploded in the aft section of the "hunter."

Unable now to press the attack, John pulled up and fired his marking rockets into the suspected SAM area before turning toward the Tonkin Gulf, sixty miles away. The Thunderchiefs fired their rockets into the area marked by the Weasel and then streaked toward the crippled F-100F to help if possible.

The Weasel was shedding parts and trailing smoke, but still flying and clawing for altitude. Captain Pitchford had managed to get the engine "Fire" light to go out by reducing power, and he was confident of reaching the water when he abruptly ran out of luck, and hydraulic fluid. No hydraulic fluid meant no flight controls, and the aircraft immediately nosed down and started gaining speed. It was time to get out!

Captain Trier ejected first with Captain Pitchford not far behind. They saw the F-100F explode below them as they descended into North Vietnam—John Pitchford to become the first Wild Weasel POW, Bob Trier, the first Wild Weasel MIA.

On 11 August 1967, the Weasels once again did a "full day's work." Place of business, the Doumer Bridge. On this occasion, Lt Col James E. McInerney, Jr., and his back seater, Captain Fred Shannon, both earned the Air Force Cross for leading a Wild Weasel flight that destroyed six SAM sites and damaged four others. Their heroic suppression efforts allowed the first Doumer Bridge strike force to complete its mission and escape without a loss. No one could ask for more.

Aerial Reconnaissance

Modern day US reconnaissance aircrews act as the eyes and ears of the commander and employ an impressive array of sophisticated aerial cameras and sensors to acquire photographic and electronic intelligence about the enemy and his environment. Reconnaissance aircraft are usually employed singly to achieve maximum surprise, in contrast to strike aircraft which are employed in larger numbers for mutual protection and to put the necessary ordnance on the target. US reconnaissance aircraft have traditionally been unarmed, partly for political reasons and partly to encourage the aircrews to avoid conflict and get the film back home. Unlike a strike mission, which is successful if the target is destroyed, a photo reconnaissance mission is successful only if the aircraft gets *back home* with the film and other target information.

These unique differences in reconnaissance employed concepts and tactics led quite naturally to the motto, "Alone, Unarmed, and Unafraid." Although the "Alone" status was to fluctuate somewhat in the course of events, and the "Unafraid" status was subject to some debate, the reconnaissance forces remained "Unarmed" throughout the Vietnam war.

Because they travel alone, or at most in pairs, reconnaissance crews can be more flexible than the strike force in attacking a target. Maneuvering prior to the target is restrained only by the enemy defenses and the crew's imagination. The moment of truth arrives when the aircraft has to be steady over the target at the proper altitude to insure photo coverage. For many, the fulfillment of this requirement proved to be the final moment of truth.

In our tale of bridge-busting, the recce crews got the photos for strike pilots to see what the target — and its defenses — looked like and then went in right behind them to document the damage. Men like George Hall and Dan Doughty in RF-101s, John Stavast/Geny Venanzi and Terry Hicks/Joe Shanahan in RF-4Cs were the unsung heroes as the "eyes of the Air Force." Unfortunately, some of them didn't get back home with the film, but their buddies who did brought many of the pictures you see in this book.

A lesser known recce function was the electronic countermeasures (ECM) mission. The EB-66 was an older bird, loaded with electronic gear, that patrolled North Vietnam's skies and jammed/suppressed AAA and SAM radars. They tuned up and, on cue, played their harmony part in the great orchestration of a bridge-busting mission.

Combat Air Patrol (MIG CAP)

Control of the airspace over North Vietnam was a major consideration in all air strikes in the country. The Combat Air Patrol, or as it was commonly referred to throughout the war, the MIG CAP, was that portion of the strike force whose sole job was to protect the strike aircraft from attack by MIG fighters.

Air strikes by the US Navy in August 1964 (in retaliation for DRV attacks on the DE SOTO Patrol) prompted the North Vietnamese into an accelerated build-up of their MIG capability. By mid-June 1965, they had received some 70 MIG-15s and MIG-17s and in December of that year were getting MIG-21s. With Russian aid, their early warning and height finding radar capability also increased rapidly. This new capability gave them ground controlled intercept (GCI) coverage over all of North Vietnam and much of the Gulf of Tonkin.

The North Vietnamese demonstrated their fighter capability early in the game when MIG-17s scrambled in defense of the Thanh Hoa Bridge on 4 April 1965. On this second US air strike against the Dragon's Jaw, two bomb-laden F-105Ds were shot down. For the early Thanh Hoa raids, protective air cover for the strike force was being accomplished by F-100Ds, armed with Sidewinder missiles and four 20mm cannons.

USAF RF-101 "Voodoo" reconnaissance aircraft at Tan Son Nhut Air Base in December 1965.

In June 1965, two Navy F-4Bs downed two MIG-17s with Sparrow missiles, the first confirmed MIG kills in SEA. The USAF then began using the F-4C as its primary MIG CAP aircraft, and, on July 10, 1965, two USAF F-4Cs downed two MIG-17s with Sidewinder missiles.

Air Refueling: The Tankers

The "gas station in the sky" was the accepted nickname for the KC-135 Strato-tanker long before Vietnam, and it was ideal for the task of refueling both bomber and fighter aircraft in SEA. The military version of Boeing's 707, it is a high-speed, high-altitude bird capable of offloading any or all of its 30,000 gallons-plus fuel capacity.

Airborne refueling in direct support of combat operations was the primary mission of the tanker force and included both pre-strike and post-strike refuelings. It also included fuel for fighters flying RESCAP (MIG cover and ground fire suppression for rescue operations), photo reconnaissance and electronic intelligence (ELINT) aircraft, and, on occasions, Navy aircraft.

The term "save" was used to reflect an air refueling with a receiver which had insufficient fuel to return to his base. In early 1965, the nickname Young Tiger was given to KC-135s refueling tactical fighters and reconnaissance aircraft in SEA. Young Tiger came to be a nickname revered by the consumer and borne proudly by the tanker crews. The "Save Scrapbook" of the 4252nd Strategic Wing contains the account of a battle-damaged fighter who was losing more fuel than the tanker was offloading to him. The tanker towed the fighter back to his base with its boom, unlatching him on final approach.

The strike aircraft used in Southeast Asia between 1965 and 1972 were fast, maneuverable, and rugged, capable of doing the job. The Thud, the Phantom, and the Navy birds, when allowed to work at full capacity, made the transport of men and material a hazardous operation for the North Vietnamese. But these planes and their courageous pilots would have been far, far less effective, if able to operate at all, had it not been for the support they received from the "gas stations in the sky," the "Wild Weasels," and the recce pilots flying their solitary missions. Between April 1965 and December 1972, Air Force and Navy strike aircraft, ably assisted by their support forces, blasted away at the Thanh Hoa and the Paul Doumer Bridges. It is this well-orchestrated effort that the Tale of Two Bridges is all about.

KC–135 refueling a flight of F–105s.

F-4 in pre-refueling position.

Chapter III. Early USAF Attacks on the Thanh Hoa Bridge

The March 1965 decision to interdict the North Vietnamese rail system south of the 20th parallel led immediately to the April 3rd strike against the Thanh Hoa Railroad and Highway Bridge, known to the Vietnamese as Ham Rong (the Dragon's Jaw). The task of planning and coordinating the mission fell to the men of the 67th Tactical Fighter Squadron (TFS), the "Fighting Cocks," commanded and led by Lieutenant Colonel Robinson Risner. Seven years later, this same 67th TFS would take the initial F-4C Wild Weasels into combat, but on 1 April 1965, the squadron was flying F-105D "Thunderchiefs" out of Korat Air Base, Thailand, and preparing to strike the Thanh Hoa Bridge.

The first punch at the Dragon's Jaw was scheduled to be thrown the morning of 2 April, but a shortage of tankers and marginal weather conditions in the target area caused the initial strike to be delayed for 24 hours. Shortly after noontime of 3 April 1965, the aircraft of Rolling Thunder Mission 9-Alpha finally climbed into the humid skies of Southeast Asia on their journey to the Thanh Hoa Bridge. This force consisted of 79 aircraft; forty-six F-105s; twenty-one F-100s; two RF-101s; and ten KC-135 tankers. The F-100s came from bases in South Vietnam, while the rest of the aircraft were from squadrons on temporary duty at various Thai bases. The ordnance loads and missions of these planes were as diverse as the fields from which they flew.

Sixteen of the forty-six "Thuds" were loaded with a pair of Bullpup missiles, and each of the remaining thirty carried eight 750-pound general purpose bombs. The aircraft that carried the missiles, and half of the bombers, were scheduled to strike the bridge; the remaining fifteen would provide flak suppression.

Seven of the F-100s were assigned to flak suppression, two to weather reconnaissance, four to provide MIG CAP, and eight were tasked for rescue top cover (RESCAP), if required. The RESCAP and flak suppression "Super Sabres" each carried two pods of nineteen 2.75 inch rockets, (The "flak birds" had two 750-pound bombs for good measure.) The MIG CAP F-100s were armed with

"Sidewinder" missiles, and the weather recce aircraft had only the 20 mm cannon ammunition which was common to all strike aircraft. The RF-101 "Voodoo" reconnaissance pilots were scheduled to obtain pre-strike and post-strike aerial photography of the bridge.

Lt Colonel Risner was designated overall mission coordinator for the attack. His plan called for individual flights of four F-105s from

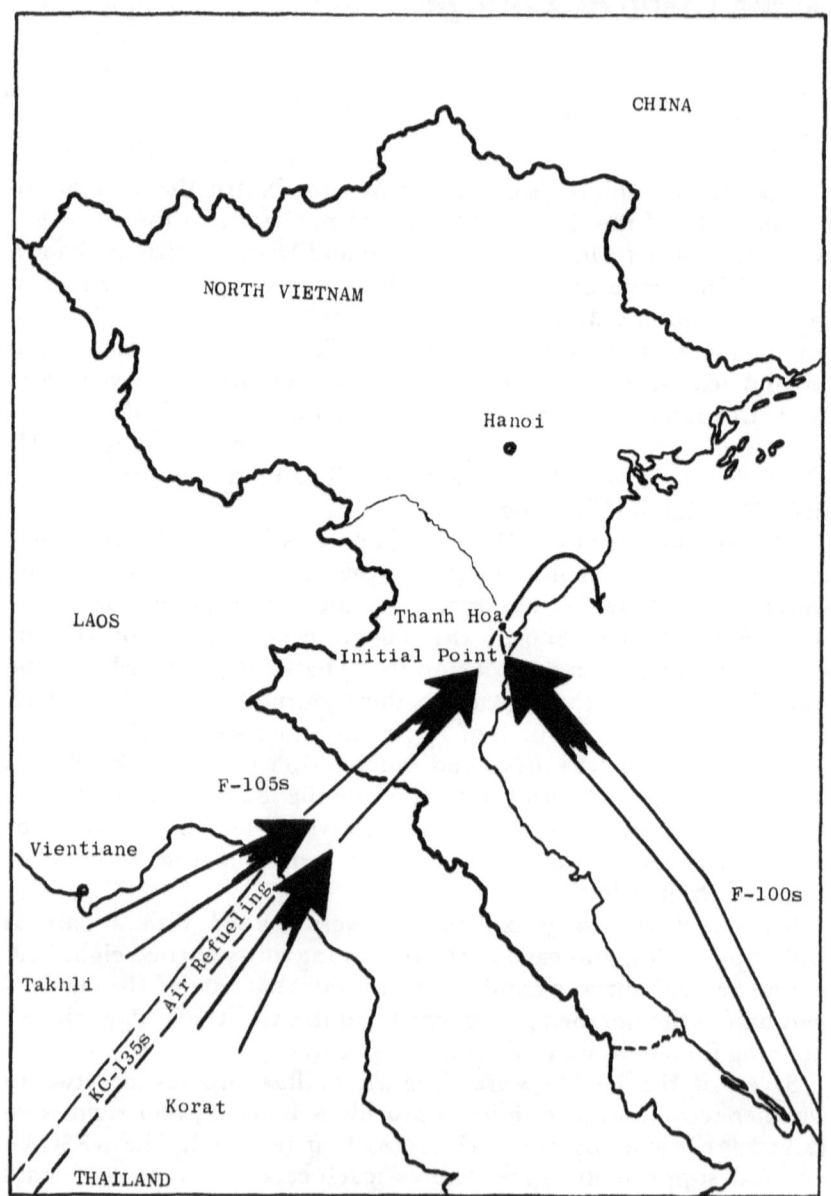

Ingress routes for the Thanh Hoa bridge.

An F-100D flak-suppressor launching a salvo of rockets at an enemy gun position.

Korat and Takhli which would be air refueled over the Mekong River before tracking across Laos to an initial point (IP) three minutes south of the bridge. Flights were scheduled to arrive over the IP only minutes apart (exact spacing depended upon the type ordnance carried) so precision timing was essential to prevent the aircraft from bunching up. The flights had to hit the IP on time and proceed directly to the attack, for it is a fighter pilot's "no-no" to hold up the aircraft behind you, especially in the target area.

The attacks would be made by proceeding north from the IP, acquiring the bridge visually, and then accomplishing a right hand roll-in to cross the basically east-west bridge at a 20° angle on a northeasterly heading. Those carrying "Bullpups" would launch their weapons at approximately twelve thousand feet, while the 750-pound bombs would be released between six and four thousand feet, with a minimum one thousand foot pull-out. This low altitude plan reflected both excessive confidence in suppression forces and a low regard for small arms and automatic weapons (AW) effectiveness at the outset of the war. In defense of the tactic, however, remember that this target proved to be more heavily defended than any previously struck, and the Thud pilots would have to press in close if they hoped to hit a target only 56 feet wide with free-fall bombs. The learning process for this generation of fighter pilots was just beginning in April 1965.

After weapon release, the plan called for all aircraft to continue east until over the Gulf of Tonkin where rejoin would take place and a Navy destroyer would be available to recover anyone who had to eject due to battle damage or other causes. After rejoin, all aircraft would return to their launch bases, hopefully to the tune of "The Ham Rong Bridge is falling down."

All the crews were thoroughly briefed on the strike plan. Strike pilots studied photos of the bridge to clarify the aiming points which were the abutments at both ends of the bridge. The destruction of either abutment would drop that particular end of the bridge into the Song Ma River. Other photos indicated that enemy anti-aircraft guns would be no heavier than 37mm.

Lt Colonel Risner's precise planning and coordination produced a clockwork-type operation, and all participants moved smoothly into place for the planned 1400 hours time-on-target (TOT). The F-100s from South Vietnam came up the enemy coast to accomplish their various support missions, while the strike force proceeded to the target area, cruising at an altitude of 17,000 feet. The sky was clear and the F-100 weather reconnaissance pilots reported visibility as five to seven miles in haze at the target.

The flak suppression sorties led the attack. Bombs and rockets were still exploding in the target area when the first flight of Bullpup carriers approached the bridge from the south and prepared to roll-

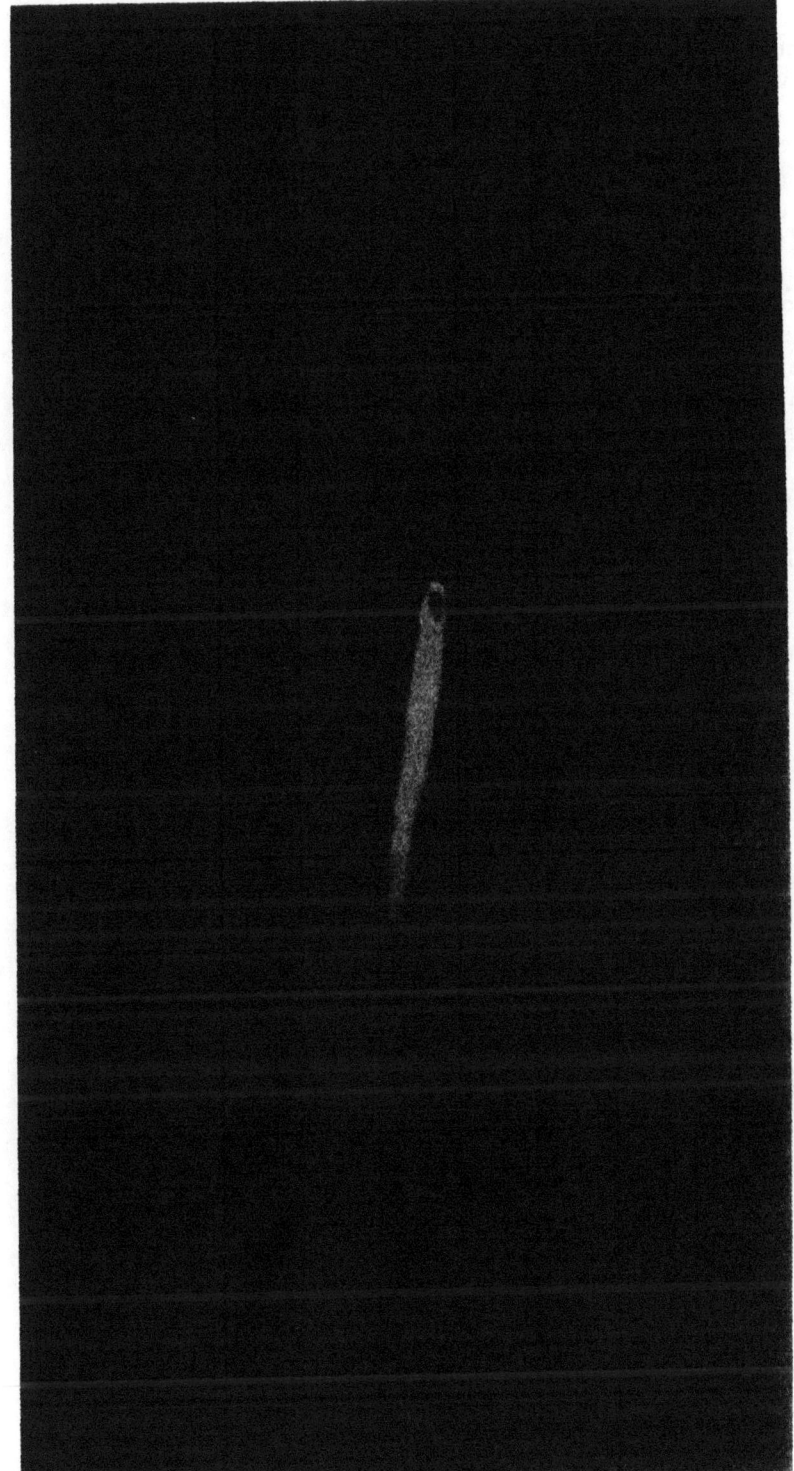

An F-105D firing an AGM-12 BULLPUP missile at the Thanh Hoa bridge.

in. The sun glinting through the haze was making the target somewhat difficult to acquire, but Lt Colonel Risner led the way "down the chute" and 250-pound missiles were soon exploding on the target. Since these missiles had to be released and guided one at a time, each pilot shooting Bullpups had to go around for a second firing pass. This second pass could slow things down considerably without the precision timing between flights.

The first two flights had already left the target when Captain Bill Meyerholt, number three man in the third flight, rolled his Thunderchief into a dive and squeezed off a Bullpup. The missile trailed bright orange fire as it streaked earthward toward the bridge. As smoke from the previous attacks drifted away from the target, Captain Meyerholt was surprised to see no visible damage to the bridge as he guided his missile to a hit on the superstructure and pulled up to go around again. Like its predecessors, his missile had merely charred the heavy steel and concrete structure. When a second attack produced the same results, it became all too obvious that firing Bullpups at the Dragon was about as effective as shooting B-B pellets at a Sherman tank.

The remaining missile attacks only served to confirm this observation. When the first of the bomb-carrying Thuds arrived on the scene, the target had barely been scratched. The bombing pilots planned to remedy this situation as they rolled their machines in on the target from 13,000 feet and then tried to keep their aircraft slowed down to the 500-knot release airspeed (the F-105 is notorious for its ability to go downhill rapidly). Hence, the 4,000 foot

Capt Bill Meyerholt who watched his BULLPUP missiles "bounce off" the Thanh Hoa Bridge.

F-105D armed with BULLPUP missiles taking on fuel prior to heading for the Thanh Hoa bridge, 3 April 1965.

minimum release altitude came up quickly, with several pilots dropping their string of eight bombs as low as 3,600 feet, only to see them hit on the far bank because of a very strong southwest wind. The last flight of the day, led by Captain Carlyle S. "Smitty" Harris, adjusted their aiming points and scored several good hits on the roadway and superstructure. Heavy smoke and haze, however, precluded any bomb damage assessment by Smitty's flight as they pulled off the target and headed for the Tonkin Gulf, but it was obvious that the bridge still stood. When Smitty looked back at the charred structure, he had no way of knowing that the smoke was really a warning from the Dragon's Jaw.

Aircraft rejoin and recovery went basically as planned, but two aircraft did not make it through the battle. Anti-aircraft fire, considerably more intense than anticipated, had claimed an F-100 flak suppressor and an RF-101. Lt Colonel Risner's Thud also took a hit just as his second missile hit the bridge. Fighting a serious fuel leak and a smoke-filled cockpit in addition to the enemy, he nevertheless nursed his crippled aircraft to Da Nang, in South Vietnam.

On this first attack, ten dozen 750-pound, general purpose bombs and thirty-two missiles had been aimed at the bridge. Numerous hits had charred every part of the structure, yet it gave no evidence of going down. Only the roadway on the south side was damaged enough to prohibit vehicular traffic. The highway on the northern side and the railroad in the center would require only minor repairs. The Thanh Hoa Bridge had suffered far less damage than its attackers had hoped for, and a restrike was ordered for the next day.

Aircrews and headquarters personnel, especially those involved with weapon planning, were disappointed and disturbed that this bridge had not fallen like those attacked previously. They did not yet appreciate that the Ham Rong Bridge had been, architecturally, grossly overbuilt. The center pillar of concrete and steel was enormous, the abutments were anchored into hillsides with reinforced concrete 30 to 40 feet thick, and most importantly, the strong single truss supported only the middle twelve feet of the bridge containing the railroad. The 22-foot highway lanes cantilevered on each side were expendable, and bombs impacting on them had little effect on the girders or the truss. Heavy weapons would have to be dropped within the narrow trussed area of the bridge to make it fall. Such a combination of weapons and accuracy was not available to the Thud pilots as they readied for the second go at the Dragon's Jaw.

The restrike was again coordinated and led by Lt Colonel Risner, but changes were made in force size, ordnance loads and tactics. This time, forty-eight F-105s would attack the bridge. Each would drop eight 750-pound bombs and the ineffective missiles were left at home for use against softer targets. The F-100s were still tasked to provide MIG CAP, RESCAP, and weather reconnaissance in the target area. However, no aircraft were scheduled for flak suppression after the previous day's futile effort.

The routing was essentially the same as the day before, so at 1057 hours on 4 April 1965, "Robbie" Risner once again turned north at the IP and began looking for the target. The low, "scuddy" clouds (and haze) dictated that on this strike the target could best be acquired if the bombing were done from east to west, still cutting diagonally across the length of the bridge. This meant the Thuds would be going away from the friendly expanses of the Tonkin Gulf during their attacks, a fact that would become most significant to Smitty Harris before the day was done.

Lt Colonel Risner once again was the first man over the bridge, but on this mission he had ordered to stay high over the battle to evaluate the effectiveness of each strike and redirect subsequent strikes. He was watching intently for enemy defensive reactions and bomb impact points when Smitty Harris, the first man down the chute, began attack number two. The pilots behind him planned to delay slightly so as to "go to school" on the initial bombs whose impact point would give a good indication of the wind correction required for accurate bombing.

Captain Harris was in a steep dive angle and could see the muzzle flashes from anti-aircraft weapons as he centered the target in his sight and pushed the "pickle button" on top of the control stick at about 4,000 feet. Smitty immediately felt his Thud lighten as three tons of bombs departed for the Thanh Hoa Bridge. Moments later, as he was pulling out of the dive at 1,000 feet and turning east toward the Gulf, a 37 mm shell slammed into the aft fuselage section of his aircraft.

The stricken Thunderchief immediately decelerated and wrenched violently to the side. The left wing fuel tank ripped away from the aircraft and Smitty was fighting for his life. Reacting instinctively, he managed to bring the disabled craft under control while fighting for altitude and trying to restart the mortally wounded engine. It was only ten miles to the water, but Captain Harris was riding a losing horse. If he had been headed toward the Tonkin Gulf when he came off the target, he might have made it. Instead, the systems warning lights were coming on one after another, the aircraft was shuddering and losing airspeed, and it was time to step outside.

The pilots directly behind the stricken aircraft could see the aft fuselage burning and coming apart, and they called for Smitty to "get out" as he disappeared into the low clouds and haze. Captain Harris never heard these calls—his aircraft radio was out and after ejection the only radio available to him was inside his survival kit. So he had no opportunity to contact anyone on the emergency net before he was captured by fifty to sixty armed peasants when he landed in a rice paddy near the target. He recalled hearing what were probably 750-pound bombs pounding at the Thanh Hoa Bridge, but the muffled roar could have been the Dragon sentencing him to over seven years in North Vietnamese POW camps!

Captain Harris was not the only pilot lost that day. Two other F-105s were shot down before they ever reached the target area. These aircraft were the last flight scheduled to strike the bridge, and they had arrived early at the IP. They were orbiting and awaiting their turn at the Dragon when four MIG-17s came out of the clouds with cannon blazing. MIGs had been seen on previous missions, but this was the first MIG attack of the war. . . and it was over almost as rapidly as it began. The enemy aircraft had used a diving, high speed pass, coming in behind the bomb-laden Thuds to nail the flight leader and his wingman. There was no chance to get even, as they continued straight ahead and out of the area at maximum speed. Both F-105 pilots were lost. The MIGs had come to protect the prestigious bridge and, in so doing, added a new dimension to what was now a rapidly expanding war.

Lt Colonel Risner, despite the historic first MIG attack, refused to be diverted from his primary mission. The Thud pilots continued to press the attack, braving a hail of anti-aircraft fire to put their bombs on the bridge—again with disappointing results.

Although over 300 bombs scroed hits on this second strike, the bridge still spanned the Song Ma River. The striking force had inflicted the maximum destruction possible considering the weapons available, and the bombs had been accurately dropped through a hail of anti-aircraft fire that, for the first time, included 57mm guns.

The bridge had been severely damaged. Both the northern and southern highways were heavily cratered and large chunks of concrete were missing. Several truss beams had been blown away and bombs had blasted right through the railroad into the river. The eastern span was sagging, but had not gone down. Extensive repairs would be required to make the bridge passable for rail traffic and the highways would never be restored to their former capability. The hard fact was that 750-pound bombs just were not big enough to deliver the *coup de grace* to such a formidable structure.

There was some consolation in the fact that the second raid did see the final destruction of several other less prestigious but, nevertheless, choice targets in the Thanh Hoa area. Primary among these was the local thermal-power plant that was seventy-five percent destroyed by well-placed 750-pounders and the aircrews mopped up by pounding a locomotive (with train) and 22 trucks into burning rubble with 20mm cannon fire. On the credit side, the bridge was sagging, a power plant was closed for the duration, plus a train and some trucks had been pulverized.

Thanh Hoa was only one target and in the overall interdiction of DRV supplies, results were in favor of the bombing campaign. The enemy was being denied his normal supply routes and the entire North Vietnamese transportation system was undergoing drastic hange. Trucks now moved only short distances and almost exclusively at night; trails were used rather than the roads; ferries substituted for missing bridges; pack animals and human supply carriers were pressed into service; and anti-aircraft guns and ammunition were being trasported along jungle trails. In effect, a completely new system, dependent on manpower, was evolving.

As the North Vietnamese reacted to the interdiction campaign, we were also learning valuable lessons that would pay dividends later in the war. Our early Thanh Hoa strikes and other USAF/USN high risk attacks contributed directly to the development of aircrew survival vests containing flares and radios, bombing tactics to keep aircraft out of the range of small arms and automatic weapons fire, procedures and formations to counter the MIG threat, new and better ordnance, and improved mission and weapon planning.

The trusty Thuds returned to the Dragon's Jaw on 7 May, just after the enemy had succeeded in making the bridge operational for rail traffic. This mission included F-4C Phantoms, armed with air-to-air missiles to oppose the new MIG threat, and electronic intelligence aircraft to confirm, if possible, the now suspected enemy use of ground controlled intercept tactics and radar directed AAA.

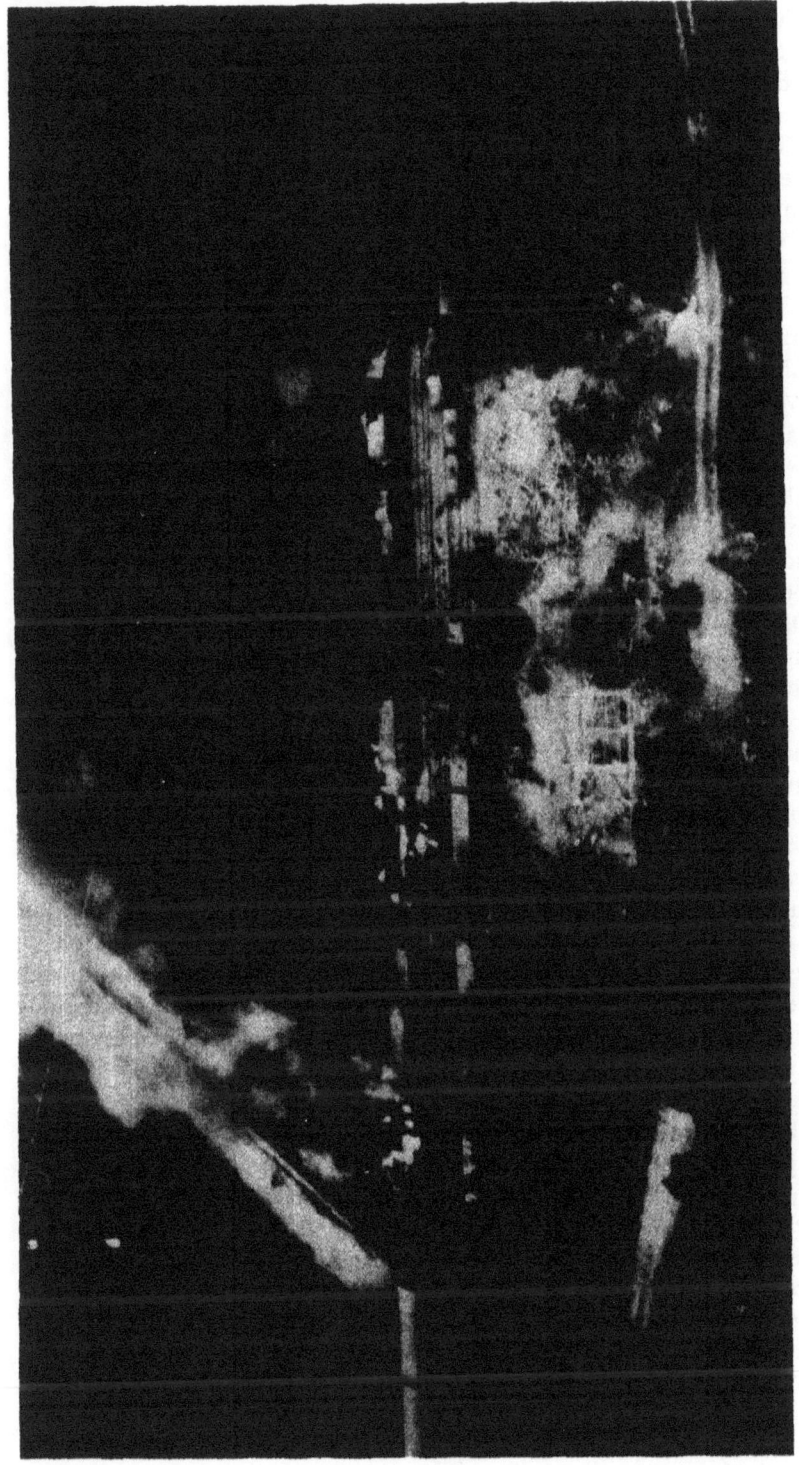

Trains trapped south of the Thanh Hoa bridge become "bonus" targets.

Twenty-eight F-105s bombed the bridge with 750-pound bombs (still the largest available), and once again the eastern span was charred, chipped, and twisted without going down. On this mission, the aiming point was changed to a point midway between the center and eastern end of the bridge rather than the abutments. As a result, the eastern approach roads and the railroad were totally destroyed by bombs that impacted just off the end of the bridge. The Dragon's Jaw was again closed for repairs. One F-105 was lost to anti-aircraft fire that now reached to 15,000 feet, but this time the pilot made it to the Tonkin Gulf prior to ejection and was rescued with only minor injuries.

Closing the Thanh Hoa bridge to traffic was just part of the overall campaign against the enemy's logistic capability below the 20th parallel. The destruction of bridges not only impeded the movement of war supplies, but also trapped large amounts of railroad rolling stock in the southern part of North Vietnam. This stranded equipment immediately became targets for armed recce [1] pilots, who seldom saw a train now that the enemy supply operations were almost exclusively at nighttime.

On one occasion, the closing of the Dragon's Jaw led directly to the destruction of 144 railroad cars and three locomotives that could not escape into their sanctuary above the 20th parallel. This significant success once again underlined the value to the enemy of the bridge at Thanh Hoa. It was the final bridge to safety in the bomb-free upper latitudes, and despite the fact that its strategic importance had seriously diminished with the effective interdiction of the rail line to Vinh, it remained a valuable target.

By mid-May 1965, a total of 27 North Vietnamese bridges had been attacked and 26 had been destroyed. Only the Dragon's Jaw remained standing and only the "Dragon" had taken its toll in American aircraft. Bullput missiles and 750-pound bombs had been quite sufficient for the French designed bridges, but were inadequate for the job at the "unengineered" Thanh Hoa Bridge. The ordnance was on target, but just wasn't designed for a bridge of this construction.

These well-delivered bombs temporarily closed the Thanh Hoa bridge each time it was struck; however, round-the-clock repair activity returned it to service each time. In light of previous strikes and losses, future attacks would require some changes. Primary among these changes was a reduction in the size of the attacking force. Flak suppression, MIG CAP, and other supporting aircraft would no longer be scheduled, and the strike aircraft would carry improved ordnance when it became available. The "Big Bullpup" with a 1,000-pound warhead and 3,000-pound bombs were to be in the Southeast

---

[1] Armed recce is a "search and destroy" mission performed by fighter aircraft.

Asia inventory by July. These large weapons could then be tested against the bridge.

The fourth Thanh Hoa mission, on 30 May 1965, was the first application of these new policies. This strike consisted on only four F-105s, which dropped thirty-two 750-pound bombs on the bridge.

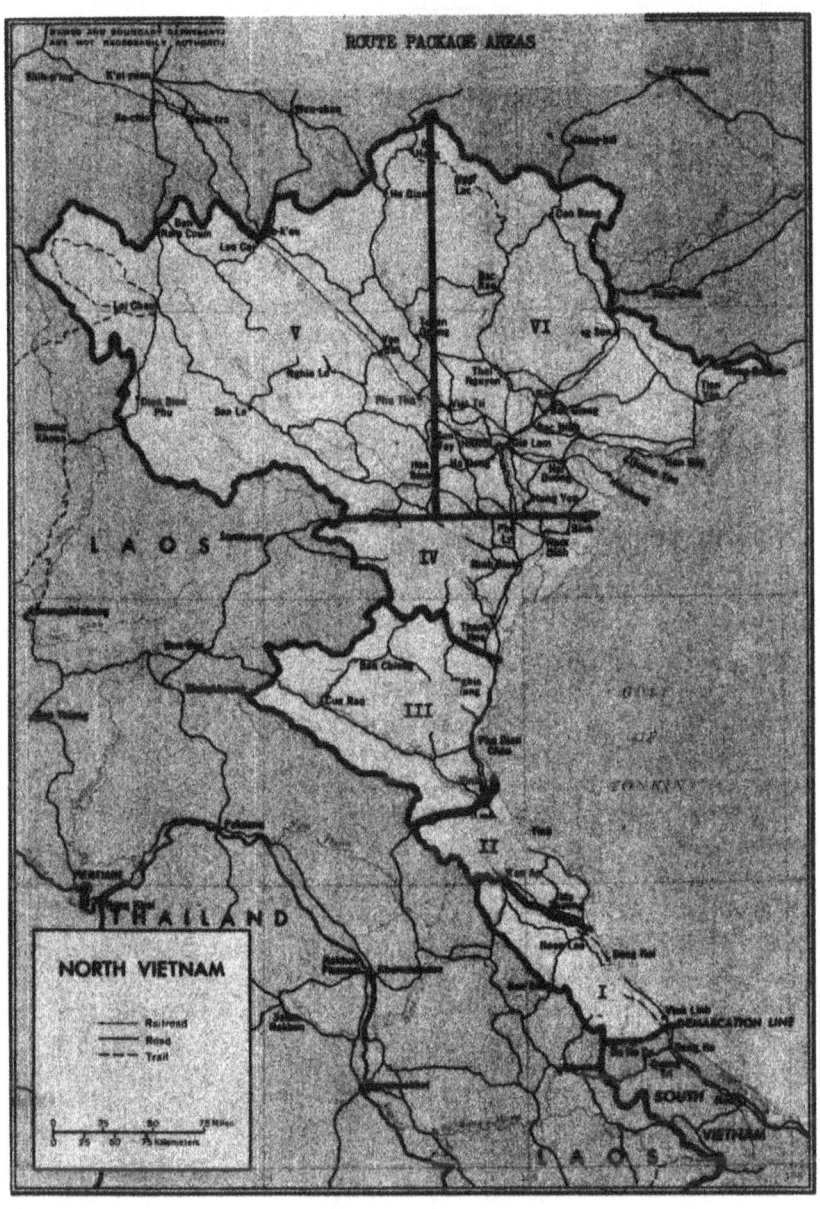

North Vietnam route package areas.

Although the bridge suffered only moderate damage, it was enough to close it to road and rail traffic. As usual, though, the bridge would soon be patched up by the North Vietnamese repair crews and another strike would be launched. By that time, it would be the Navy's turn since the Route Packaging System, initiated in November 1965, assigned Route Pack IV, with the Thanh Hoa bridge, to the men and machines of Carrier Task Force 77.

Chapter IV. Three Long Years

From the beginning of hostilities in 1964, coordination of the air interdiction effort against North Vietnam by the USAF and USN had been a subject of some interest at all levels of command. Because of differences in operational concepts, procedures and equipment, a formal USAF/USN command and control system was not immediately established which could allocate available air resources against the enemy in efficient, coordinated joint air operations. In the early periods of the war, the US Navy launched its air operations from two aircraft carriers off the cost of North Vietnam in an area called "Yankee Station," while the USAF flew from bases in South Vietnam and Thialand. In mid-1966 the Navy added a third aircraft carrier to Yankee Station operations.

As the numbers of daily sorties increased, the authorized target list expanded, the enemy's defenses grew stiffer, and it became increasingly clear that something would have to be done to provide more control of the TAC-air operating over North Vietnam. CINC-PAC and CINCPACFLT had delegated authority for day-to-day planning and conduct of the armed recce portion of Rolling Thunder to the Commander 7th Air Force and the Commander, Task Force 77. They, in turn, had established a Rolling Thunder Armed Reconnaissance Coordinating Committee (RTARCC), later redesignated RTCC. This committee's charter was to resolve and coordinate items of mutual interest to the Navy and Air Force, to insure optimum effectiveness of the Rolling Thunder program through elimination of overlapping areas of interest, and to reduce duplication of effort against North Vietnamese targets.

Inasmuch as the previous system had been less than satisfactory to both services, RTCC, in November 1965, divided North Vietnam into six areas called Route Packages (RP) and each service was given primary armed reconnaisance responsibility in several of these RP's. The USAF and the USN were allotted three packages apiece. From the inception of the Route Package System, the Thanh Hoa Bridge, which lay in RP IV became the responsibility of the US Navy. As we shall soon see, the Navy was to expend considerable air effort against the bridge with much the same results as the earlier Air Force attacks.

Navy Strikes the Thanh Hoa Bridge

The aircraft carriers operating on Yankee Station had fewer aircraft available for interdiction efforts against North Vietnam than the USAF. The number and type of aircraft carriers operating on "the line" varied throughout the conflict, but a typical carrier had about 70 attack and support aircraft on board. Primary attack aircraft used by the Navy against the Thanh Hoa Bridge included A-4 Skyhawks, A-7 Corsair II's, A-6 Intruders, F-4B Phantoms and, on occasion, A-3B Skywarriors and F-8 Crusaders. These planes delivered vast amounts of ordnance on the bridge in an effort to deny its use by North Vietnamese trains and trucks. Bombs varying in size from 500 pounds to 2000 pounds, and missiles with warheads as large as 1000 pounds of TNT were hurled against the Dragon's Jaw time after time. The results were twisted girders and temporary closings of the bridge.

On 17 June 1965, the Navy began a three-year effort to destroy the bridge. Attacking the target with small strike forces of two to four aircraft, the Navy hit the bridge some 24 times with a total of 65 aircraft between June 1965 and the end of May 1966. The ordnance dropped during this period was approximately 128 tons.

This lack of success in not being able to drop the bridge completely should not be construed as a lack of capability, initiative, or professionalism on the part of the aircrews involved; but rather it is an acknowledgment of the intrinsic strength of the bridge itself. The experts now realized that weapons in the 2000 and 3000 pound class would be required to drop the Thanh Hoa Bridge. Both concrete highways had been destroyed by repeated bombings, thereby eliminating approximately 40 feet of a 56-foot wide target. Thus, the placing of a bomb on a 16-foot wide, 500-foot long steel bridge from a fighter aircraft traveling over 500 mph while being fired on by a myriad of AAA weapons became a monumental task! Day and night strikes against the bridge, using visual as well as radar bombing techniques, had succeeded only in shaking the steel girders. The approaches to the bridge, however, were battered to the point where, according to one Navy official, "The general area looks like a valley on the moon."

The North Vietnamese, in addition to expending a great deal of manpower and effort on repairing the Thanh Hoa, also built pontoon bridges in the vicinity to provide a by-pass while the bridge was unusable. While this effort was a tribute to the tenacity and dedication of the North Vietnamese people to keep their lines of communication (LOC) open, it also represented a desired ancillary effort from an interdiction campaign. The more manpower and time required by the enemy to keep his LOCs open, the fewer people there were available for farming, industrial work, and other vital tasks necessary to keep the war machine in the homeland running.

USS Constellation operating in Gulf of Tonkin.

A-3B Skywarrior bombing North Vietnam.

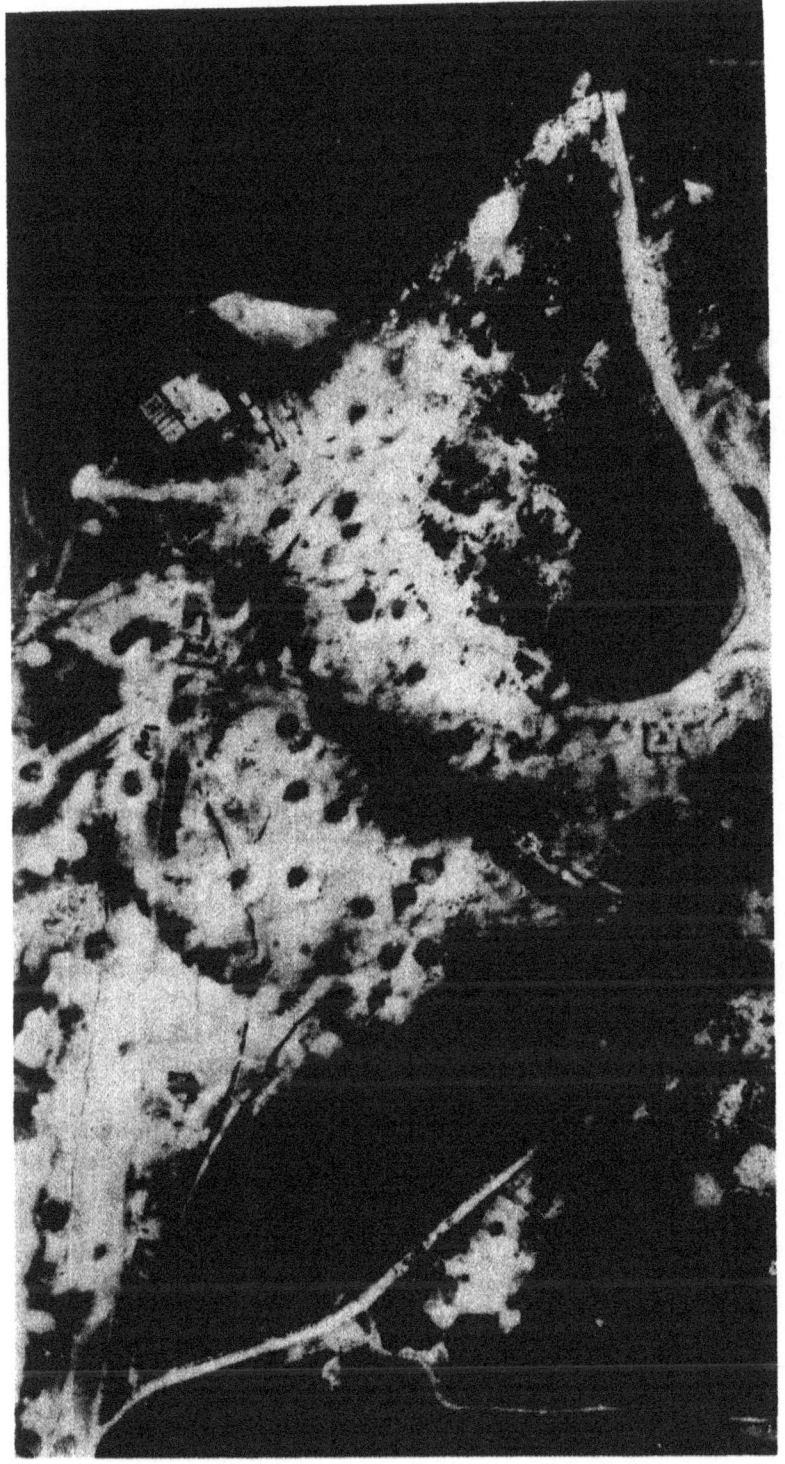

The approach to the Thanh Hoa Bridge (Valley of the Moon).

The proximity of the Thanh Hoa bridge to the Gulf, some eleven miles inland, together with the normal weather patterns over the northern part of North Vietnam, combined to provide very poor weather over the target much of the year. Low cloud ceilings and fog greatly hampered air operations against the bridge. Smoke from burning fields and a continual haze were additional hazards in trying to locate and destroy the bridge. This combination of heavy clouds and poor visibility put the pilot in a very precarious position to combat the radar-controlled SA-2s and AAA since the ability to elude a SAM depended upon the pilot seeing it and taking evasive action at the appropriate time. AAA is also evident by the puffs of smoke left by exploding shells; therefore, forces were not sent against the bridge unless weather conditions were such that the pilot's ability to maneuver and evade were unimpaired.

In some seasons of the year, poor weather permitted only 2-4 visual attacks per month. This, of course, worked to the enemy's advantage inasmuch as he was able to carry out of great deal of repair work and thus keep his LOCs open for long periods of time.

Defense Continues to Improve

When the air activities started over North Vietnam in 1964, enemy defenses were sparse to nonexistent. This, however, was soon to change in the Thanh Hoa area. By 1966, AAA was being moved into the area in increasing numbers and the North Vietnamese Air Force was beginning to flex its muscles. In early January 1966, the first sighting of a MIG-21 occurred 90 miles east of Thanh Hoa and a second MIG was pursued by US fighter aircraft 25 miles southeast of Thanh Hoa at a low altitude. This was the beginning of the North Vietnamese Air Force's efforts to extend its operational ring and frequency of flights over the Gulf of Tonkin and away from the Hanoi area. Although the US had lost two F-105s to MIGs in April 1965 over Thanh Hoa, very lttle had been seen of MIGs that far south of Hanoi.

It became obvious by early 1966 that the North Vietnamese were being liberally supplied with vast amounts of AAA. Before the December 1965 standdown, only one mission in twelve—8 per cent—had been engaged by North Vietnamese anti-aircraft fire. However, by late February 1966, AAA defenses had increased to the point that one mission in four was being engaged and this was to increase dramatically before the war ended.

A part of this rapidly expanding AAA and MIG threat was a more sophisticated radar-controlled environment which was capable of providing the range, altitude, speed, and azimuth of US aircraft to enemy gunners or pilots. To counter this new enemy capability, US

This SA-2 anti-aircraft missile (SAM) site (above) was photographed in the vicinity of Thanh Hoa, North Vietnam. SA-2 site (below) in vicinity of Thanh Hoa Bridge.

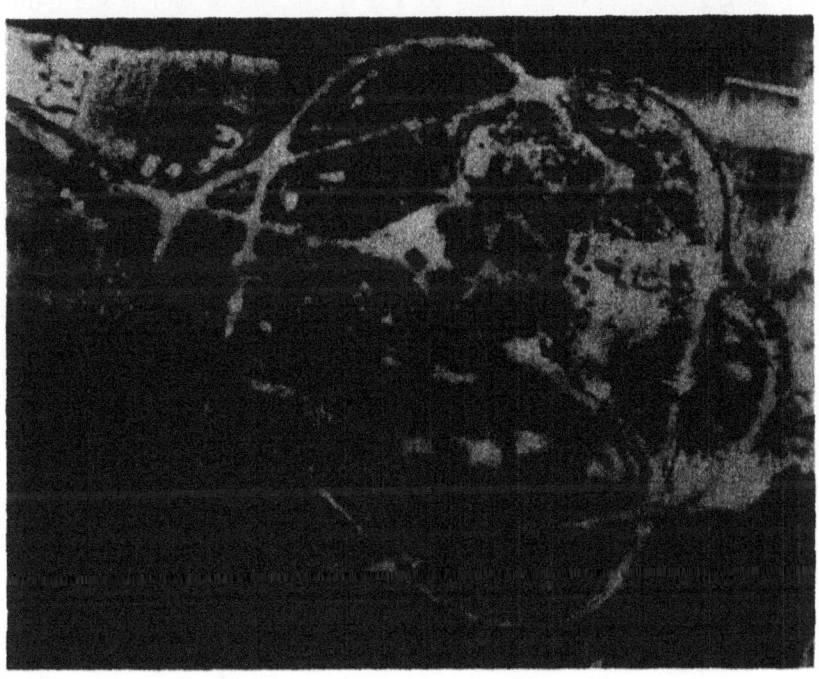

forces designed and employed a new flak suppression weapon — cluster bomb units (CBU) — which proved highly successful. Electronic countermeasures were refined to make it extremely difficult for the North Vietnamese to use their radar systems without encountering jamming. On it went, counter for counter, until the war was terminated some years later.

Interdiction of the Thanh Hoa-Vinh Rail Line

While efforts were being made to destroy the Thanh Hoa Bridge, attacks were continually flown against rail line RR#4, which ran south from Tahnh Hoa to the city of Vinh. Since the bridge had not been destroyed, it was imperative that rail traffic not be allowed to move south of Thanh Hoa. It was impossible to prevent all supplies from getting through to the south, so interdiction became a matter of making it as difficult, expensive, and time-consuming as possible for the enemy.

RR#4 was struck repeatedly in early 1966, obliging the North Vietnamese to rely on trucks for transportation. In May 1966, four trucks were destroyed by air strikes on highway on highway 1A, five miles south of Thanh Hoa. Photographs of the results of this strike showed 169 inactive units of rolling stock in the vicinity of Thanh Hoa due to damaged rail lines and highways. Restrikes were immediately launched from the carriers against the trapped cargo, causing great losses of rolling stock and supplies to North Vietnam. By mid-June 1966, RR#4 had been interdicted in thirteen places south of the Thanh Hoa Bridge, and rail traffic was brought to a standstill.

Although the enemy was catching hell along RR#4 during the first six months of 1966, the fact remained that the Thanh Hoa Bridge was still intact. The apparent invincibility of the bridge; its cost in men, aircraft, and ordnance, its potential strategic importance; its symbolic value to the North Vietnamese — all served as an incentive for US aviators to find different techniques to destroy it.

Project "Carolina Moon"—(May 66)

One innovative effort took shape in September 1965. At that time personnel at the Armament Development Laboratory at Eglin AFB, Florida, came up with the concept of mass-focusing the energy of certain high explosive weapons. The applicability of this concept to new weapon designs was proved in many exhaustive experimental tests in the Eglin complex. Lieutenant General Moore, Commander of the 2nd Air Division in Saigon, was informed of the new mass-focus weapon and its potential against bridges, particularly against the Thanh Hoa Bridge. The new weapon, however, was rather large and would have to be delivered by a cargo type aircraft. General Moore felt that attrition would be high if cargo aircraft were used directly against the Thanh Hoa Bridge. He responded by suggesting that methods of upriver delivery be studied.

As the development of the weapon progressed, it became evident that delivery by C-130 aircraft was feasible and the Tactical Air Warfare Center (TAWC) was directed to form and train an appropriate task force. The weapon, in its final configuration, would weigh 5,000 pounds and resemble a large pancake about 8 feet in diameter and 2-½ feet thick. The design was such that the weapon was detonated initially around its periphery with the resultant force of the explosion focused along the axis of the weapon in both directions. The weapon was to be floated down the Song Ma River where it would pass under the Dragon's Jaw, and detonate when sensors in the bomb detected the metal of the bridge structure.

It sounded like a bold plan — and it was. Specialists in many fields were called upon to solve problems associated with extraction techniques, chute deployment, drop accuracy, and river transit of weapon affected by such things as depth and current of the river, position of the tide, and wind draft on its exposed surfaces. This was a formidable task, but acceptable solutions were found and the plan proceeded.

Two C-130 crews and supporting personnel were sent to Eglin AFB for intensive training and preparation for the upcoming mission. The first crew was led by Major Richard T. Remers; the second by Major Thomas F. Case. Quite simply, the plan was to drop five weapons one to two miles up river from the bridge under the cover of darkness. Entry and exit over the North Vietnamese terrain would be at less than 500 feet to avoid radar detection. The route selected was about 43 miles long, which meant the aircraft would be over enemy territory for at least 17 minutes.

To assist in masking the approach of the C-130, a flight of two F-4 fighter aircraft was scheduled to make a diversionary attack, using flares and bombs, on the highway 10 miles south of Thanh Hoa shortly before the C-130 was to drop its ordnance. In addition, a EB-66 was tasked to carry out jamming in the area during the attack period. The plan was firm, the crews were selected, and training began at an accelerated pace. Training sites in the Eglin area, which had radar returns similar to those anticipated during the 17-minute flight over North Vietnam, were selected.

Their training completed, the two C-130 crews and aircraft deployed to Danang AB on 15 May 1966. Along with the necessary maintenance and munitions specialists, ten mass-focus weapons were provided, allowing for a second mission should the first one fail to accomplish the desired results. The last of the contingent arrived at

Danang on 22 May 1966 and began their final preparation for this unique assault on the Dragon's Jaw.

Last minute changes made on the route to the target included intelligence up-dates on automatic weapons and anti-aircraft artillery positions, as well as a review of checklist and rescue procedures. In this regard, an interesting discussion developed between the two crews. Major Remers felt that the aircraft was tough enough to survive moderate anti-aircraft artillery hits, and gain enough altitude should bail-out be necessary. Major Case agreed that the aircraft could take hits, but the low-level flight would preclude a controlled bail-out situation. With these conflicting philosophies, and the fact that either parachutes or flak vests could be worn — but, not both — Major Remers decided that his crew would wear parachutes and stack their flak vests on the floor of the aircraft; Major Case decided that his crew would wear only flak vests and store the parachutes!

The first strike was scheduled for the night of 30 May, but on 27 May, intelligence detected a five-fold increase in AW sites and five new AAA sites. However, a re-evaluation of the plan showed it to be secure and the mission was "on."

Major Remers and his crew took off from Danang at 25 minutes past midnight, turned out over the water at 100 feet altitude and headed north under radio silence. Within an hour, he had guided his bird to the coast-in point in North Vietnam. Maintaining an altitude of 100 feet above the water to avoid enemy radar detection, the big four-engine Hercules crossed the coast of North Vietnam and headed for the bomb release point. Two release points had been selected in the river; one was two miles and the alternate, one mile from the bridge; it was left to Major Remers and his two navigators, Captain Norman G. Clanton and First Lieutenant William "Rocky" Edmondson, to detect the actual drop point.

As they approached the first drop zone, Major Remers climbed the aircraft to 400 feet and slowed to 150 MPH. Having encountered no enemy fire, he elected to press on to the closer drop zone. Shortly after passing the first release point, heavy, intense AW and AAA fire was encountered, but it was too late to turn back. Fortunately, the ground fire, although intense, was inaccurate and missed the C-130 by several hundred feet. The five weapons were dropped successfully in the area closest to the bridge. Immediately after the drop, Major Remers banked his "Herky-bird" sharply to the right, dove back to 100 feet above the ground and made for the safety of the Gulf of Tonkin. The operation has gone flawlessly! The diversionary attack south of Thanh Hoa went as planned and, although it drew an unfriendly reception, both F-4's returned to Thailand unscathed.

Mission effectiveness could not be assessed until the photo reconnaissance birds made their run at dawn. Needless to say, the crew felt

Major Remers' crew immediately after mission: Kneeling: 1st Lt William R. Edmondson, navigator; Capt Norman G. Clanton, navigator; SSgt Aubrey B. Turner, loadmaster; A3C Johnny A. Benoit, loadmaster. Standing: MSgt John R. Shields, flight engineer; 1st Lt Thomas M. Turner, co-pilot; Maj Richard T. Remers, aircraft commander.

the mission was personally successful — they had survived.

Pent-up emotions of the crew gave way to excited activity by all involved in the project as they waited for the recce report. Unfortunately, the pictures revealed no noticeable damage to the Thanh Hoa Bridge nor were any of the bombs seen along the edge of the river. Intelligence could find no trace of the bombs and a second mission was laid on for the next night, 31 May. The plan for Major Case's crew was basically the same with the exception of a minor time change and slight modification to the route of flight.

A change in crew was made at the last minute when Major Case asked "Rocky" Edmondson, the navigator from the previous night's mission, to go along on this one because of his experience from the night before. Ten minutes after its planned 1:00 AM takeoff, the C-130 departed Danang, turned out over water, and headed north. The aircraft and crew were never seen or heard from again.

The flight of F-4s was making its diversionary attack at the designated time when one of the F-4 crews saw anti-aircraft fire and a large ground flash in the vicinity of the Thanh Hoa Bridge approximately two minutes prior to the scheduled C-130 drop time. Photo reconnaissance the next morning revealed no wreckage and an intensive search and rescue mission was flown over the Gulf of Tonkin with no results. Moreover, one of the two F-4 aircraft was shot down that evening and its crew was never recovered. With the unsuccessful conclusion of this second mission, the remaining C-130, its crew, and support personnel redeployed to the United States and the mass-focus weapon was not used again in Southeast Asia.

Some time later, a North Vietnamese PT boat crewman was taken prisoner, and during his interrogation he revealed that in May 1966, a US aircraft dropped five mines in the river near the Thanh Hoa Bridge. Although four of the five mines exploded, there was little damage to the bridge.

In June of 1966, Major Remers saw communist film footage from a Japanese source on a major US evening news program which showed the North Vietnamese parading what he recognized to be parts of a C-130. Additionally, the North Vietnamese stated that none of the Americans on board the aircraft had survived.

Strikes Continue Through 1966

The weather in RP IV was so poor during the early months of 1966 that the Navy flew only eleven bombing sorties against the Thanh Hoa Bridge, just enough to keep the rail approaches to the bridge in bad shape. As the weather began to clear in the summer months, more and more effort was expended against the Dragon's Jaw and the lines of communication north and south of the bridge. The pressure and accuracy of the air strikes severely limited the supplies the North Vietnamese could trasport on Highway 1A and RR#4. This successful interdiction of the LOC south of Thanh Hoa caused the enemy to shift his southern LOC westward to Route 15 which put his supply route closer to Air Force interdiction operations.

On 23 September, the Thanh Hoa Bridge was struck by 22 Navy attack aircraft which dropped 57 tons of ordnance and rendered the bridge unserviceable once again. Some 80 units of rolling stock and 1678 tons of POL, trapped in the Thanh Hoa area, were systematically destroyed during a four day period. The North Vietnamese supply effort had been dealt a blow.

Clearing weather allowed the US air effort to expand over the North Vietnamese heartland and with it came changes in the NVN defense system. By July 1966 SAM firings had increased six-fold over the month of June. The North Vietnamese changed their missile tactics by firing two missiles at once, fuzing them for different altitudes. In addition, missile launch procedures were varied; the missile was sometimes fired with the guidance radar in "standby" until the missile entered its final phase of flight, when the guidance radar would be turned on and signals sent to the missile to intercept the aircraft. This procedure deprived US pilots of precious seconds of reaction time in evading the missiles.

Despite these and other tactical changes, AAA remained the greatest threat to US aircraft. As a pilot took evasive maneuvers to escape the deadly SA-2, he would turn hard and head for the ground, thereby defeating the missile which could not turn as fast. However, as the aircraft descended to lower altitudes, it entered the lethal envelope of the heaviest AAA environment in all aerial warfare. So it was a combination of SAMs and AAA that the pilot had to contend with, and anything less than complete attention to the situation at hand often spelled disaster.

In October 1966, photo reconnaissance missions revealed little or no activity in the repair of the bridges and rail facilities along RR#4 south of Thanh Hoa. No airstrikes were flown against Thanh Hoa during this time. However, in December 1966, photo reconnaissance revealed increased tempo in repair activity along the rail lines, bridges, and rail yards. This called for renewed action against the rail lines as well as the bridge itself. Thus the strikes went on, day after day, week after week, with notable success against the LOCs but powerless to knock out the bridge.

The Walleye Glide Bomb

Several strikes were flown against the "Dragon" during the first few weeks of 1967, but with the same disappointing results. In January 1967, however, a US Navy aircraft carrier departed San Diego, California, carrying a new generation of weapons into the Vietnam conflict, the Walleye Glide Bomb, one of the new "smart bombs." The Walleye is a free-fall glide bomb with a 1000-pound warhead which has in the nose a TV camera designed to track and impact on a high contrast aim point the camera relays what it sees to a scope in the cockpit through which the pilot identifies the target. The pilot sights the target on his scope, positions a set of crosshairs over the pre-selected contrast point, identifies this point to the Walleye, and releases the bomb within its glide and guidance parameters. The key significance of this new weapon is its pinpoint accuracy. It also furnishes a limited stand-off capability, which allows the pilot to release the weapon farther away from the target than is possible with conventional bombs.

In early March 1967, plans were made to attack the Thanh Hoa Bridge as soon as possible with the new Walleye. Missions were flown on 11 March, using the Walleye against military barracks and small bridges to familiarize the pilots with actual weapon employment. Results of these strikes were so successful that the Commander, Carrier Division, Task Force 77, scheduled a Walleye mission against the Dragon's Jaw on 12 March. Attack Squadron 212, designated for this strike, had been provided with a scale model of the Thanh Hoa Bridge to be used in conjunction with a movable light source (simulating the sun) to locate the best points of contrast and the time of day these conditions would occur. Army demolition experts

Thanh Hoa Bridge immediately after a daylight attack.

also were on board the carrier to assist in identifying the most vulnerable spots on the bridge structure and the sun's contrasting effect, the pilots and demolition experts agreed that 1412 hours (2:12 pm) on 12 March would provide maximum contrast for the chosen aim point.

The sun shone brightly on 12 March as the pilots rode the escalators from their ready rooms to the flight deck. Although there was a considerable number of AW and AAA sites protecting the Dragon, the strike force for this mission consisted of only three A-4 Skyhawks, with one Walleye each, and two F-8 Crusaders for MIG protection. The mission was planned so that each aircraft would make individual runs on the bridge from south to north in order to give the pilot as much time as possible to locate the aim point, identify it to the weapon, and release it. The flight was launched and joined up over the carrier prior to heading for the target. Enroute, the pilots completed their checks on the weapons systems and declared the mission a "Go."

Over the target, each pilot dove at the bridge at 500 mph and released his weapon as planned. Initially the AW and AAA was very light, but when the third pilot initiated his run, the enemy fire was extremely heavy. As the pilot searched for the aim point, he could see, in his peripheral vision, hundreds of flashes on the ground which he knew all too well to be the enemy guns firing at him. With the aim point sighted, identified to the weapon, and "bombs away," all three pilots headed their Skyhawks toward the Gulf of Tonkin. Photography taken from the strike aircraft showed that all three weapons impacted within five feet of each other on the designated aim point; but, the bridge still stood. This mission was to be the final glide bomb mission against the Dragon until some five years later. Subsequent Walleye missions against other North Vietnamese bridges were highly effective as each bridge attacked was put out of commission. The Navy also dropped 68 more Walleye Glide Bombs against barracks, power plants, and bridges scoring 65 hits in the process.

Limited Strikes Through 1967

After the Walleye attack in March, the weather closed in again and prevented further strikes until late April, when the low monsoon clouds began to disappear. Once more the Navy took on the Dragon in an attempt to destroy one of the last remaining enemy strong points. Although the bridge had been damaged many times in the past and the North Vietnamese had paid dearly in men and materiel to keep it open, it had become a paramount symbol of North Vietnamese determination. Defenses continued to be increased around

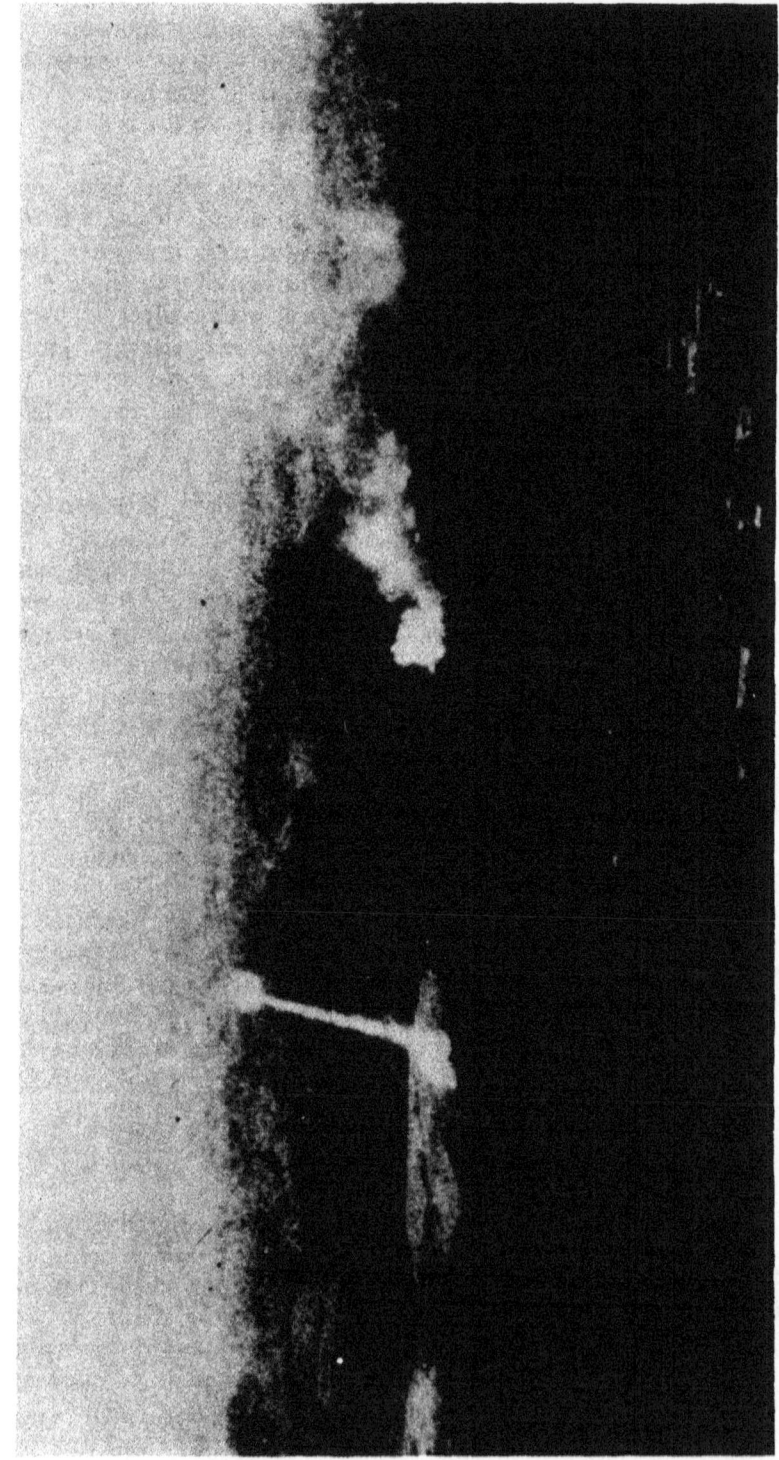

SA-2 missile launched toward American aircraft over North Vietnam.

A-4 Skyhawk armed with two SHRIKEs and two WALLEYE glide bombs.

Thanh Hoa and the SAM missiles, now more numerous, were causing much concern. Furthermore, the North Vietnamese were developing new tactics to coordinate the use of their MIGs, SAMs, and AAA in a single area—new methods that were soon analyzed and countered with improved equipment and new tactics by the Americans. From late April 1967 until the end of September 1967, the Navy flew 97 sorties and dropped approximately 215 tons of bombs on the bridge.

The weather turned bad again in October and so severely hampered air efforts against LOGs in RP IV that aircraft targeted

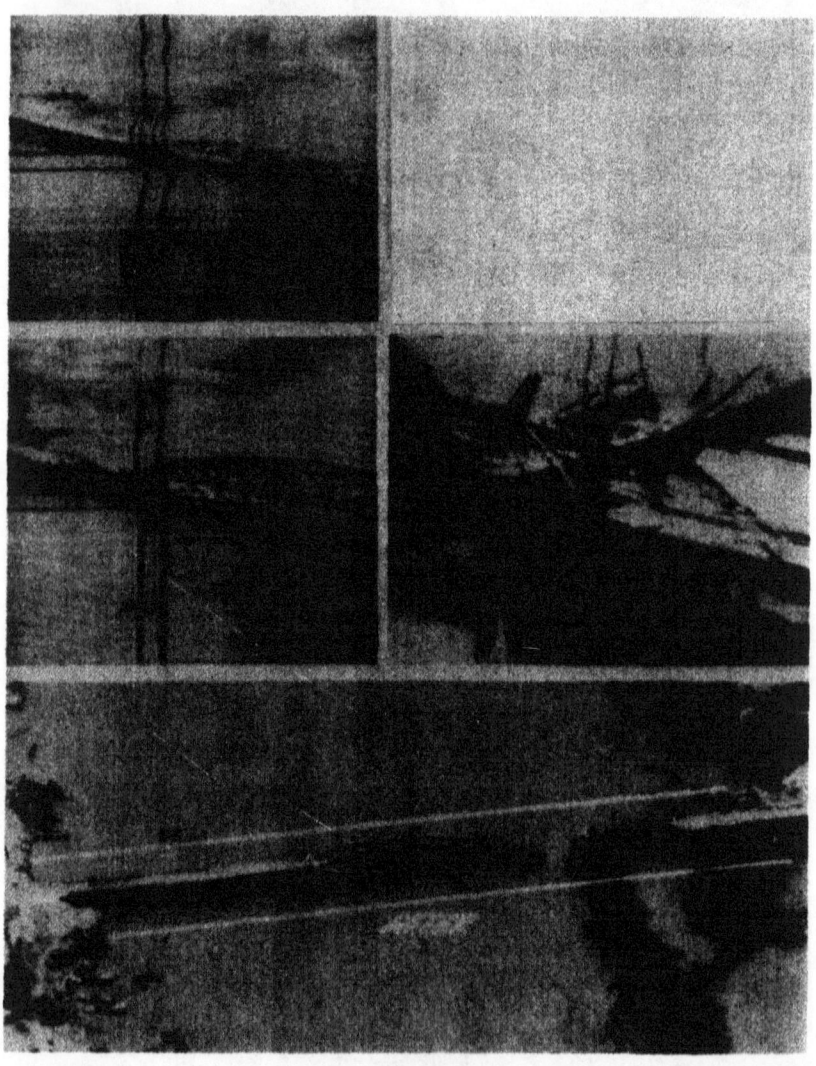

Composite (four pictures) showing destruction of Ninh Binh railroad/highway bridge by WALLEYE bomb.

against the Thanh Hoa Bridge were usually sent to RP VI or to Laos to expend their ordnance. This was the pattern of operations until late January 1968; when the weather around Thanh Hoa cleared for a few days.

A Big Strike Ends the First Round (28 Jan 68)

Intelligence and reconnaissance showed signs of increased efforts by the North Vietnamese to repair their south-bound LOCs during the bad weather period. Reasonable immunity from US air strikes during that time helped the enemy put a good deal of his LOCs in working order again. This factor along with the US high command's knowledge that negotiations might lead to another bombing halt provided the impetus for a coordinated USAF/USN air strike against the Thanh Hoa Bridge. Optimism ran high that this time the bridge would be felled by the largest attack on the Dragon's Jaw since April 1965. At 0500 on January 28, US Navy A-4 Skyhawks hit the bridge and over the next 3-½ hours, 44 Navy and Air Force fighters hurled themselves at the bridge, dropping about 3 tons of bombs on the bridge every 4-½ minutes. Again it was a day of frustration for the American pilots. Photo reconnaissance pictures showed only superficial damage to the superstructure of the bridge, although girders were twisted and bent. The southern approach to the bridge was severely damaged. Rail tracks, twisted and torn, lay astride the rail bed which was no longer recognizable because of large bomb craters. The harsh truth was a bridge temporarily unusable, but one that would be operational again in the future. Soon after this mission, bad monsoon weather once again enveloped the bridge in low louds, rain, and poor visibility which saved it from further bombing.

Bombing Halt Comes in Early 1968

The United States had been attempting for some time to bring the Vietnamese conflict to an honorable and just conclusion. Its efforts had been directed in many directions and involved many countries in attempts to find a solution which would allow the South Vietnamese to exist and govern themselves without interference from their northern neighbor. In early 1968, it appeared that the climate and conditions for political negotiation were favorable. Thus encouraged, President Johnson halted all bombing north of the 19th parallel on 31 March 1968. This order by the Commander-in-Chief was to shield the Dragon's Jaw from further military attacks for many years to come.

Bomb hits on Thanh Hoa RR Ferry 21 Sep 1966.

Navy F-4 being catapulted off the aircraft carrier USS America in the Gulf of Tonkin on 3 Sep 1970.

By 31 March 1968, a number of changes had taken place in the physical appearance of the Dragon's Jaw. The formerly massive structure—a central railroad flanked by concrete highways—was now a charred, dented, and twisted maze of steel girders. The central rail bed had become a patchwork of flimsy boards upon which rested twisted and bent tracks. Both approaches to the bridge were so cratered that the movement of vehicular traffic was impossible. During the next four years, however, substantial repairs would make the bridge again functional and a key target in the second round.

Chapter V. The Paul Doumer Bridge Goes Down

"They got a little place just south of the Ridge, Name of the place is the Doumer Bridge..." So goes the "Doumer Bridge Blues" written by Bill Middleton about the air war over North Vietnam. The story which follows recounts the events of 1967-68 during which US airmen wrote an exciting chapter in the history of airpower. It is the story of the destruction of the Paul Doumer Bridge in the heart of North Vietnam.

The Paul Doumer Bridge was almost as important symbolically and more important militarily to the North Vietnamese than was the Thanh Hoa Bridge. For US airmen, it was a major prize in the effort to stem the tide of supplies moving into South Vietnam. Destroying it would mean much: a morale boost for our own side, shock and dismay to the enemy, and hope for those who were POWs in the hated Hanoi Hilton.

There was an important difference between the Doumer and Thanh Hoa bridges: the former had never been attacked because it lay within an area near Hanoi which the US had chosen to leave untouched between 1965 and 1967. In the summer of 1967, however, US leaders finally decided to attack targets within and near Hanoi. The new target list, Rolling Thunder 57, contained six targets within a ten-mile radius of downtown Hanoi and the Doumer Bridge had a high priority on that list. Thus, the stage was set for a major effort against the North Vietnamese transportation system, and the Doumer Bridge became a prime target.

The word was flashed to the field and preparations were made to carry out Rolling Thunder 57. The planners, in making their analyses, noted the differences between the Thanh Hoa and Doumer Bridges, and gave careful consideration to the lessons learned from strikes on Thanh Hoa. One of the most important lessons was the significance of choosing the correct weapon. Military planners decided that the F-105, carrying 3,000 pound bombs, would bear the brunt of the effort against the bridge.

The 7th Air Force headquarters planners, known as the "Alpha" team, in response to a directive from General Momyer, 7th Air Force Commander, prepared the necessary directions for the field units operating against the Paul Doumer Bridge. The 355th TFW at Takhli, the 388th at Korat and the 8th at Ubon, all Thailand-based tactical fighter wings, were selected as the strike forces against this target. Directions were encrypted and dispatched to each of the wings at 1000 hours on 11 August 1967. The go-ahead had come through the system from Washington, the weather was good . . . the time had come to go after the Paul Doumer Bridge.

Missions to be flown on a given day were ordinarily directed from higher headquarters the previous day so that the munitions/maintenance personnel would have adequate time to prepare the proper bomb loads, fuel the aircraft, and load the electronic equipment. Thus, when the new directions came in early on the 11th, the aircraft had already been prepared for the targets selected on the 10th. Maintenance and weapons crews were ordered to reconfigure the aircraft with 3,000-pound bombs in place of the 750-pounders already aboard. Normally about one-hour-per-aircraft was needed to change the fuel tanks and bomb loads—but not on this day. Taking calculated risks, the commander temporarily waived the rules prohibiting the loading of fuel and munitions simultaneously, and the normal one-hour aircraft task was compressed into 18 minutes. The entire operation went flawlessly—morale was sky high since all the personnel involved appreciated the importance of the new target.

The 355th TFW would lead the three wings against the Doumer Bridge. The excitement of "going downtown" (the popular phrase used by pilots for missions to Hanoi) permeated the wing. Colonel (now Major General) John Giraudo, the Wing Commander, and Colonel (now Major General) Bob White, Deputy Commander for Operations—both highly experienced combat veterans from WWII and Korea—quickly assembled the aircrews. It was evident that this target would require all the expertise available. Colonel Giraudo had just arrived in the theater, so he designated Colonel White as Force Commander and mission leader. For the other 19 airplanes in the Tahkli force, they selected the most experienced men available in the wing to go on the raid.

The pilots hurriedly prepared maps in accordance with guidance received from the Alpha team, and filled out line-up cards, complete with call signs, aircraft tail numbers, code words for success, etc. Then, the briefing process began. Systematically, crews synchronized their watches with a "time hack" from the operations officer. Code words used for various purposes were reaffirmed. The weather officer provided a detailed account of conditions enroute, in the target area, and what could be expected on the return to base. The route would be clear all the way with only light winds in the target area—an almost perfect setting for the attack. The intelligence officer provided target information, particularly the desired munitions impact points. The crews were informed that the defense environment would include 37, 57, 85 and 100mm guns, AW, SAMs, and MIGs—the entire array of enemy capability.

Following the overall briefing, the men in each flight of four Thuds discussed the specific tactics they would use under varying circumstances. Some of these topics were the rules of engagement, anti-MIG tactics, SAM evasion, and downed air-crew procedures. In many ways, this resembles the last-minute huddle before a big game.

The crewmembers quickly donned flying suits, "G-suits," helmets, gloves and other paraphernalia and, in the personal equipment room, survival vests were checked. Small two-way rescue radios, now carried in the vests to preclude the problem Smitty Harris experience at Thanh Hoa, were checked and rechecked. Water bottles were filled and stuffed into pockets, and a .38 caliber pistol loaded into a shoulder holster. The crews grabbed their parachutes, jumped into the flight line vans, and headed for their aircraft. The time was approximately 1300 hours.

On the flight line, the ritual of aircraft pre-flight inspection was conducted. Personal equipment was placed in the cockpit (parachute, helmet, clipboard, maps, photos, and cards). Munitions were double checked, especially the bomb fuses which were set to detonate the bombs the instant they came in contact with the bridge. The safety wire, extending from the bomb to the bomb rack to protect against detonation while on the airplane, was secured and checked. With a time-on-target of 1558, all preparations had been worked backward so that start engines would be precisely at 1350 and takeoff at 1418. Watching the aircraft start, taxi, marshall, arm, takeoff, and join-up, was like watching an orchestration of men and machines.

All activities were tuned to perfection and went precisely like clockwork including the graceful, almost eerie movement, of a "25-ton canary" (so aptly painted on the side of one F-105) as it glided through these motions. Later, the mission would be jokingly referred to as a "triple pumper," a term so often heard when crews relaxed and the incessant movements of hands was evident in describing what had happened on a tough mission in North Vietnam.

Water injection was used for take-off, with 11-second spacing between aircraft. This gave maximum performance for the aircraft as they labored in the hot 93 sun, becoming airborne in 28-29 seconds after a ground roll of just over one mile. The lead aircraft accelerated to 300 knots, flew approximately three miles on the runway heading and then began a slow, lazy 180 turn to allow his flight members to begin checking and double-checking all systems, for if one aircraft was not functioning correctly in any way, a space (there were airborne and ground spare aircraft) was ready to replace it. This day, however, all was well with not one abort—ground or air.

Photo of Doumer Bridge in May 1968, a month after the bombing halt.

The spares returned to the flight line to wait for another day, another mission.

Air refueling took place over Northern Laos at what was called "Green Anchor." The fighters in each flight with the least amount of fuel at initial join-up received fuel first, so that if anything was wrong with an aircraft's refueling system, the pilot could divert to a friendly base with sufficient fuel to recover safely. In this way minimum time and effort were expended on the refueling.

At approximately four minutes prior to departure from the tankers, each fighter began to "topoff" his tanks with those precious last few gallons needed to be absolutely full. After topoff, each flight departed the tankers in unison, joined the other flights, and headed north. As usual, the tanker crews had performed their mission perfectly—no hitches, minimum radio calls, and precisely the correct time and position at the conclusion of refueling.

The strike force that day consisted of a Wild Weasel flight, one flak suppression flight, three bomb flights, and cover, consisting of one F-4 (8th TFW) MIG CAP flight. Each flight contained four aircraft.

After crossing into North Vietnam, all flights "greened-up", a term meaning all switches were set so that appropriate munitions were ready. The Wild Weasels were out in front carefully scanning, listening, and looking for SAM's, MIG's, and radar directed AAA as the strike force made its way in brilliant sunlight toward downtown Hanoi. As the force crossed the Red River, approximately 95 miles Northwest of Hanoi, and simultanelously increased speed from 500 knots to 0.9 mach (nearly 600 knot), altitude was about 10,000 feet. At four minutes to go, the force turned the corner at the northwest end of "Thud Ridge." [1]

The gauntlet of defenses would now be tested. Those beautiful but deadly little puff clouds of flak from guns of various calibers would soon begin to appear. At this point, variations in altitude would be made to confuse the gunners and evade the flak.

As the force proceeded southeast along Thud Ridge, MIGs were taking off from Phuc Yen airfield, only a few miles from the strike force flight path, and were soon making arching, climbing turns in a vain attempt at a head-on intercept. The force plunged through their midst without loss or damage. To make a 180 turn and catch the Thuds would now be impossible for the MIGs—they simply could not catch up in time.

As the strike force came off the east end of Thud Ridge, the target appeared clearly. It stood out like a black snake spanning the

---

[1] Thud Ridge was the name given to a prominent limestone karst outcropping that ran northwest from Hanoi. It was a rugged range and provided a natural, mountainous region over which one could fly relatively unhampered by ground defenses.

Two F–105 Thunderchiefs enroute to enemy targets stand by as a third refuels from a KC–135 tanker.

brownish turbulent waters of the Red River; it looked just like the intelligence briefers said it would.

Time was short as the last turn was made to the south and climb was begun to 13,000 feet for the bomb run. The pilots called this climb the "pop" for the roll-in. It was a maneuver wherein a flight could evade flak, climb to the bombing altitude, and position all four aircraft into echelon formation. Then, at precisely the correct point over the ground calculated to produce a 45° dive angle for the final run, aircraft 1 and 2, followed by 3 and 4, would commence their roll-in and dive-bombing run.

During the bomb run, the aircraft were pointed at the ground, and aimed at the target with engines oftimes operating in the afterburner range. All the while, each wingman was flying formation just off the wing of his leader — a neat trick, but one which any good fighter pilot learns to master.

The flak was very thick; the 85mm guns were firing as rapidly as they could and a number of SAM missiles were fired. It was the show the pilots had been told to expect and it lived up to its billing.

The bomb run lasted less than seven seconds: seven seconds to fly the aircraft to the exact spot in the air for bomb release — seven seconds after hours of preparation and flight to the target — seven seconds to the moment of truth — the longest seven seconds in the world as flak hurtled past on all sides!

On the north side of the river, west of the bridge, was an 85mm site with seven guns. The flak suppression flight completely destroyed it — it simply went up in smoke! On the southeast side of the bridge, another 85-mm site survived and its guns poured their deadly stream of red-glowing balls of steel but none struck, although the fireballs could be seen going by. Perception, the ability to perceive all this and yet concentrate on the target and fly formation, is only possible after years of training and strict self discipline. Perception is a trademark of the USAF fighter pilot and proved its worth over and over again during the long Vietnam war. Stacking the line-up with veterans paid off. The winds were from 350 degrees at six knots, so only a minor correction was needed to keep the aircraft lined up properly on the target. The first flight's leader, flying at 550 knots, released bombs at 8000 feet as planned, but his wingman made one last correction, had the aircraft exactly where it was needed, and released bombs at 7000 feet. Speed brakes went in, pull-up initiated, and a hard left turn executed down river to the east. The strike pilots were now overflying the "Hanoi Hilton" and their former flying mates would know they had been there that day because they were flying at supersonic speeds and the boom noise would confirm their presence. As the lead flight maneuvered to the east, Number Two, looking back at the bridge, saw a span drop into the water. His heart was really racing now — they'd done it! "Giraffe" would be the code word flashed back for all the world to know — SUCCESS!

Two aircraft were damaged that day, Bear Four and Marlin Three. Of course, the favorite propaganda artist, Hanoi Hannah, who broadcast daily over short wave radio from North Vietnam, would exaggerate their losses.

Bear Four took a direct hit in the afterburner section from an 85mm shell. His aircraft burst into flames — it was torching. The pilot shut off the afterburner, the flames went out, and he called for assistance from his flight mates. The remaining members of Bear flight located their ailing comrade south of Hanoi and escorted him to Udorn, Thailand, where he landed safely. The landing gear collapsed on touchdown, but the pilot walked away uninjured. The flight surgeon with the ground rescue crew got a real shock when the pilot of Bear Four emerged. . . John Piowaty had a red handlebar moustache that definitely ended the flight surgeon's claim to the longest handlebar moustache in Southeast Asia.

Marlin Three took a 57mm hit. Pieces of the shell penetrated the aircraft's front and right windscreen, some hitting the instrument panel. The aircraft also received a one-inch hole on the right side of the nose. However, the pilot was not injured and recovered his aircraft safely at Takhli.

The 8th and the 388th Fighter Wing forces, attacking several minutes behind the 355th, dropped two highway spans into the Red River.

As the aircrews returned to home base, went through maintenance debrief, and headed for the debriefing, it became apparent that a major success had been achieved that day.

Recalling the day's action, Lt Col Harry W. Schurr, 469 TFS, described how the flights rolled in and how all hits appeared to be right on the bridge, with the 3,000-pounders popping like big orange balls as they struck. Capt Fred Shannon, 388th TFW Weasel, contributed his description of how the Weasels knocked out two SAM sites to insure the safety of the strike aircraft.

Congratulatory phone calls came into Colonel Giraudo's office from the force leaders at Ubon and Korat. The strike photos below (reproductions from 16mm color strike camera film) confirmed in living color what the aircrews had reported. The bridge was cut and span was down. Photos taken by a lone RF-4C moments after the last strike aircraft was gone from the target confirmed the strike crew pictures.

The following message is indicative of the reaction at higher headquarters:

> "From Commander, 7th Air Force Lt Gen Momyer, Personal from Gen Momyer to Col Giraudo (355th), Col Olds (8th) and Col Burdett (388th). Subject: Mission of 11 August 1967. The

superb execution of the strike yesterday on the Hanoi Railroad and Highway Bridge was a display of the finest bombing and teamwork witnessed to date in the SEA conflict. All participants in this mission demonstrated capability and professionalism. As you are aware, execution of this operation has the attention and interest of the highest levels of government. My sincere congratulations to you, the airmen officers of your entire organization."

A recap of the first raid on 11 August 1967 reveals thirty-six strike aircraft (those that actually dropped bombs) from three wings participated, led by the 355th at Takhli. They dropped 94 tons of bombs and destroyed one rail span and two highway spans on the northeast side of the bridge. The superstructure was damaged and the highway portion on the north side of the bridge, where it crossed the island in the river, was cut. This stopped the movement of an average of 26 trains per day with an estimated capacity of 5,950 short tons. Two aircraft were damaged, but no pilots were lost. The heart of the North Vietnamese transportation system had been dealt a severe blow.

By 30 August 1967 photography showed the bridge to be under repair and estimated completion-time was three weeks. A rail ferry, located about 3.5 nautical miles southeast of the bridge was being used for limited service. By 3 October 1967, the bridge was restored for both rehicular and rail traffic.

The monsoons brought bad weather to North Vietnam once again and in so doing helped the Vietnamese by preventing US attacks on the bridge. It was not until 25 October 1967 that a break in the weather made it feasible to attack. At that time, 21 F-105s dropped 63 tons of 3,000 pound bombs. Again the bridge was rendered unserviceable by the destruction of 2 cantilever span just east of the island, the eastern pier supporting the span, and the highway deck on the span just west of span number 5.

The bridge was repaired and serviceable by 20 November 1967. Again, weather caused delays in bombing until 14 and 18 December 1967, when clear skies permitted 50 F-105s to drop ninety-plus 3,000 pound bombs. On 14 December, the rail and highway decking was cut between the 6th and 7th spans from the east side and the decking damaged on the 2nd and 3rd spans. On 18 December, the 2nd, 3rd, and 4th spans and half of the 5th span were damaged. It was estimated that it would take 2½ to 3 months to repair the damage enough to handle traffic. In fact, it was not until 14 April 1968, when a 2800-foot rail bridge (pontoon type), 4.5 nautical miles southeast of the Doumer Bridge, was completed, that rail traffic again flowed across the Red River by other than ferry.

In all, 177 sorties (carrying 380 tons of ordnance) were flown against the Doumer Bridge during 1967-68. 113 were F-105 strike sorties, with F-4 and other aircraft providing flak suppression and MIG CAP. Additional support came from F-105F Wild Weasel.

An aircraft on ingress and egress to this target area could expect to encounter fire from over 300 anti-aircraft gun positions and approximately 84 SAM sites, each with 4 to 6 launchers. 109 SAMS were fired at US aircraft and 24 MIG 17/21 aircraft were encountered. Two US aircraft were lost to anti-aircraft fire and 15 were damaged.

On 2 January 1968, photography revealed the following condition of the 19 span bridge: four spans still down, three damaged beyond

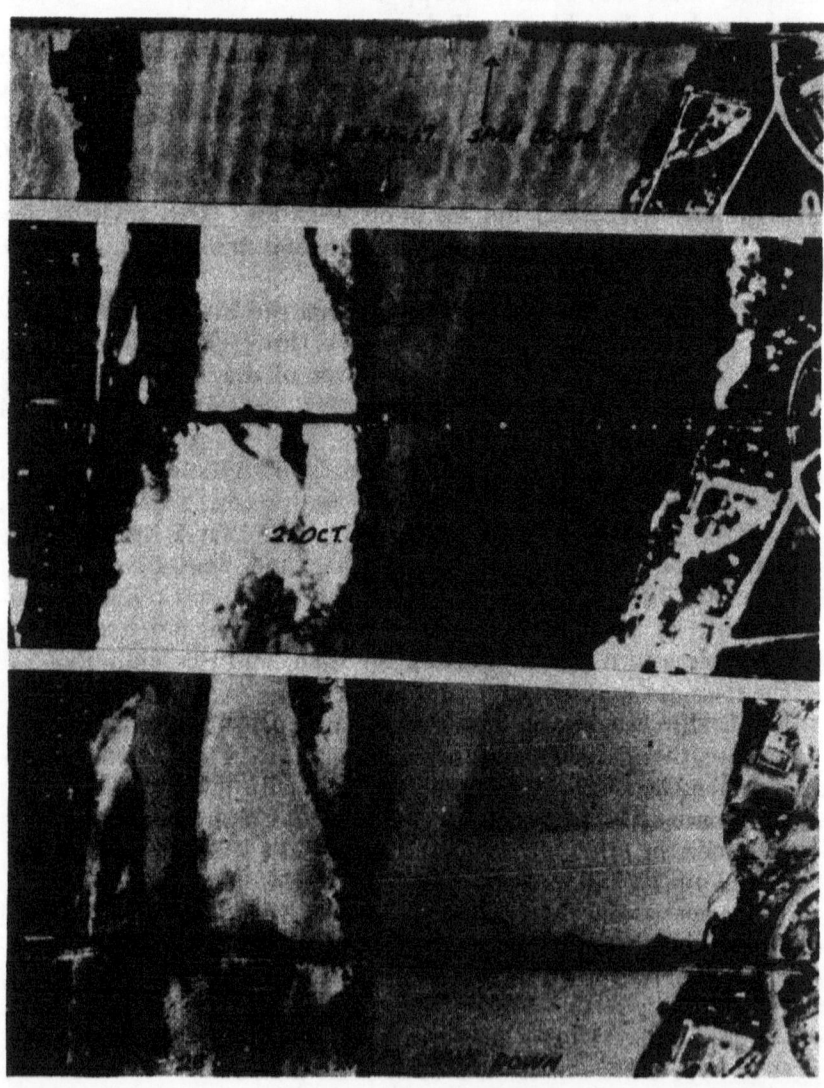

Sequence of three pictures showing the different stages in the destruction of the Doumer Bridge (Aug 11, Oct 21, and Oct 25 in 1967).

use, 12 were restored, and two permanent main piers and one temporary pier destroyed. It was estimated that 2½ to 3 months would be again needed to repair the bridge.

From that time until the 31 March 1968 limited bombing campaign, bad weather precluded hitting the bridge again. Further bombing probably would not have been necessary, considering the condition of the spans and the time needed to repair them. The limited bombing precluded all activity above 20 North and permitted rebuilding of the Doumer Bridge. In 1972, US aircrews would again attack it as a prime target, only this time they would use guided munitions to write yet another exciting chapter in the history of the airpower.

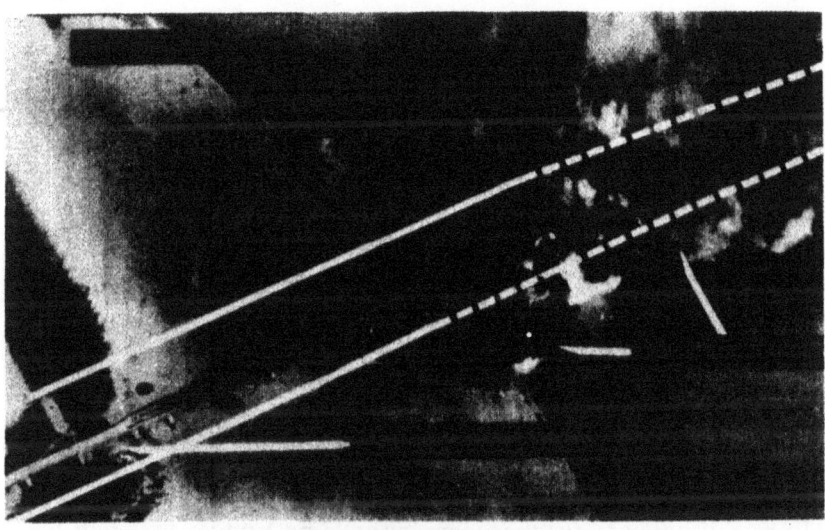

Strike and post-strike photos of Doumer Bridge, 18 Dec 1967.

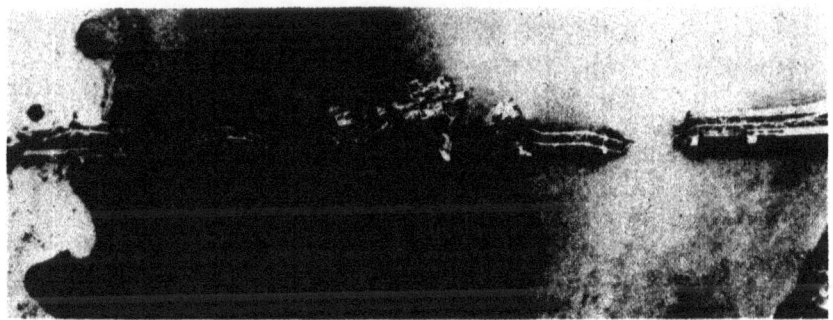

Chapter VI.   Both Bridges Fall

The Bombing Halt (1968-1972)

One of the most significant dates in the Vietnam war was 31 March 1968. On that day, Lyndon B. Johnson announced that he "would not seek, nor accept," the nomination for another term as President. Following this, he ordered a halt to the air and naval bombardment north of 20° North Latitude and called upon the North to enter into peace talks to end the war. President Johnson's action received widespread praise around the world as a major initiative for peace. Although it denounced the continued bombing below 20 North, Hanoi was quick to accept the "peace talks" offer and declared its readiness to arrange a meeting of representatives. Thus began a four-year period that was to prove one of the most frustrating and devisive in American history.

Shortly after the first bombing restriction, President Johnson further restricted the bombing to south of 19 North, making the Thanh Hoa bridge immune to attack. On 1 November 1968, the President ordered a halt to *all* bombardment of North Vietnam. During "bomb free" 1969, the transportation system throughout North Vietnam operated at full capacity and the input to the Ho Chi Minh trail network reached new highs. The bridges that had been destroyed or damaged before 31 March 1968 were repaired and traffic was again heavy.

Meanwhile, in the rest of Indochina, withdrawals of US troops continued. More aggressive action by the Viet Cong and North Vietnamese operating form sanctuaries in Cambodia, convinced President Nixon that the safety of remaining American troops would be jeopardized if the sanctuaries remained. Thus, during May and June, the allies eliminated the Cambodian sanctuaries with a massive ground offensive well supported by air power.

During the four years of the bombing halt, American fatalities in the war had increased by over 25,000 and stood at 45,679. During the same four years, however, President Nixon's "Vietnamization" policy had reduced U.S. forces in South Vietnam from more than 540,000 to approximately 70,000 men. On 30 March 1972, nearly four years to the day after President Johnson's initiative for peace, the North Vietnamese launched their biggest invasion of the war, attacking across the DMZ into Quang Tri province. U.S. tactical air power in Thailand was employed to stall the offensive while units that had gone home were redeployed to SEA. USAF squadrons of F-4s, F-105s, EB-66s, KC-135s, and B-52s were deployed to Thailand, South Vietnam, and Guam. Additional U.S. Navy aircraft carriers were returned to the South China Sea. By the end of July, the largest air armada of recent years had been assembled. Once again, the systematic aerial bombardment of North Vietnam was underway the transportation system and the bridges were key targets.

Doom for the Dragon

When the North Vietnamese invaded South Vietnam on 30 March 1972, it became painfully obvious that Hanoi had no desire to accept any settlement other than one dictated by a smashing military victory. On 6 April 1972, American aircraft once again were sent north of the DMZ to carry out a coordinated interdiction campaign against the North Vietnamese logistic network. Two of the targets were the Thanh Hoa and Paul Doumer bridges. Since the bombing halt in 1968 they had been repaired, and the rail lines crossing the bridges were being fully utilized.

It was clear to the targeteers, mission planners, and strike pilots that destroying the Thanh Hoa and Doumer bridges would not be a simple task. They had taken their toll of US aircraft and pilots during the early years of the war, and there was no reason to suspect that the defenses around them had been softened. There was, however, a glimmer of hope echoing along the halls and in the briefing rooms of the fighter squadrons because some new weapons were now available for such a mission.

A new family of "smart bombs" had been introduced in Southeast Asia since the bombing halt in 1968. These weapons consisted of Electro-Optical Guided Bombs (EOGBs) and Laser Guided Bombs (LGBs) in the 2,000-pound and 3,000-pound class. The EOGB was a contrast weapon, similar in concept to the Walleye first used in 1967 by the US Navy. The EOGB, however, was a 2,000 pound bomb with a small TV camera attached to the nose which transmitted a picture of what it was viewing to a scope in the attack aircraft. The pilot would point the aircraft and weapon at the target area thereby allowing the Weapon Systems Operator (WSO) in the rear cockpit of the F-4 to find the target on the scope, refine the contrast aiming point and designate the target to the weapon. Once this was accomplished, the pilot would release the bomb and quickly depart the target area, leaving the EOGB to guide itself toward the designated aim point. Target weather and cloud cover was a factor

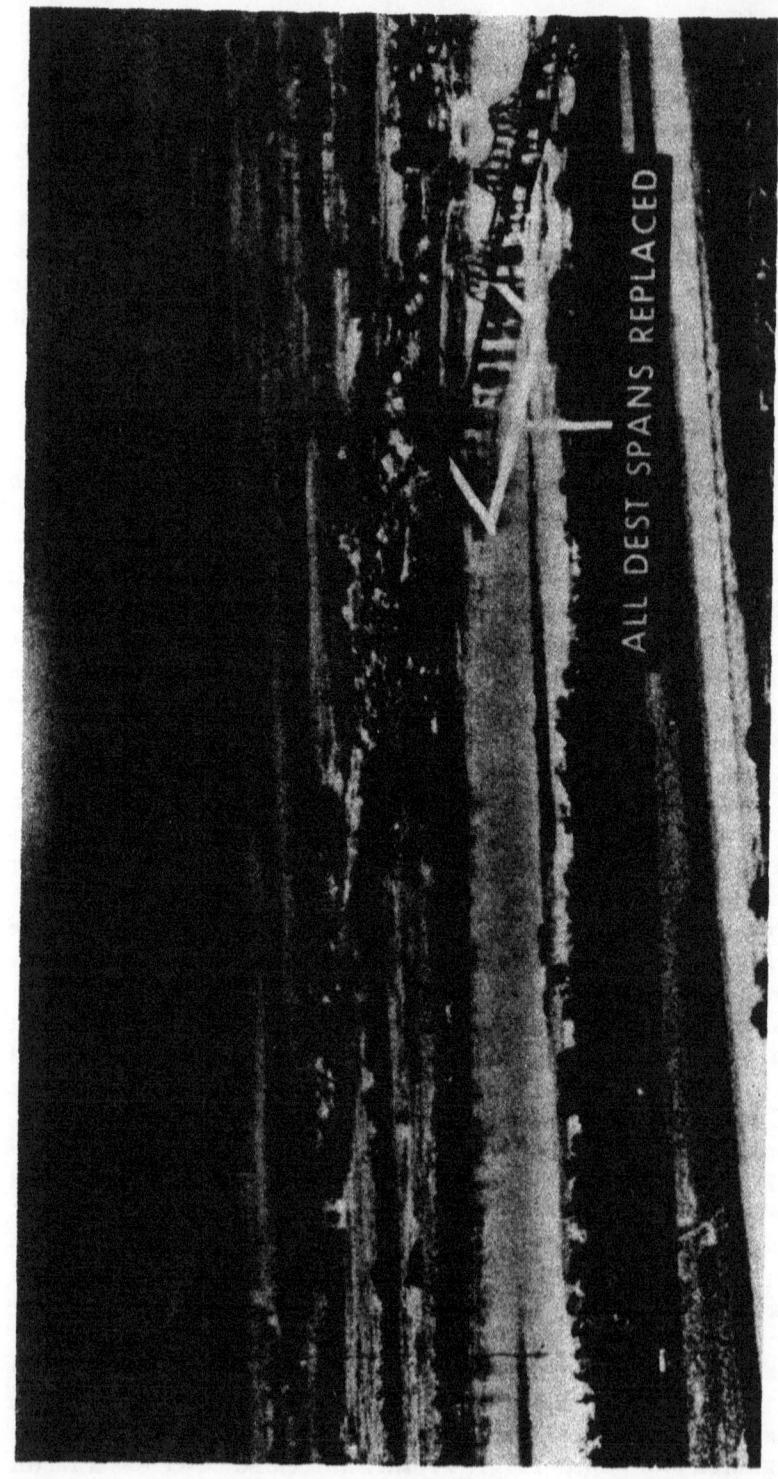

A sequence of photos showing the rapid restoration of the Doumer Bridge following the 31 March 1968 bombing halt.

An F-4E with a 20mm cannon in the nose and carrying two Laser Guided Bombs (LGBs).

when delivering EOGB's, but if the weapon could see the target when it was released from the aircraft it would usually impact the aim point.

The LGB was somewhat different. A laser sensor was mated to the nose of a 2,000 or a 3,000-pound bomb which enabled it to guide itself toward a target illuminated with low power laser energy. The problem of illuminating the target with this laser energy was solved by attaching a pod beneath the fighter aircraft. This pod contained an optical viewing system and laser emitting capability, both operated by the WSO in the backseat of the fighter. With this system, the pilot could point his aircraft toward the target while his WSO optically located the precise target aim point and illuminated it with his laser equipment. The pilot would then release his bombs and depart the target area leaving the LGB to guide itself to the target. An advantage of this system was that more than one aircraft at a time could drop LGBs on the same target, with all weapons using the same illumination point to guide on. Both the EOGB and the LGB resulted in less aircrew exposure and greater accuracy than conventional weapons. A disadvantage was that the target had to be continuously illuminated by the laser for the LGB to be effective. If clouds obstructed the view of the illuminating pod the LGB would become an unguided bomb and probably miss the target.

The new EOGBs and LGBs were given to the 8th Tactical Fighter Wing (TFW) operating F-4 Phantoms from Ubon Royal Thai Air Base, Thailand. By April 1972, the F-105 Thunderchief strike aircraft had been replaced in Thailand by the newer, more modern Phantoms. The 8th TFW was known as the "Wolfpack MIG Killers"—a name acquired for their effectiveness in destroying more MIG aircraft during Rolling Thunder than any other US tactical

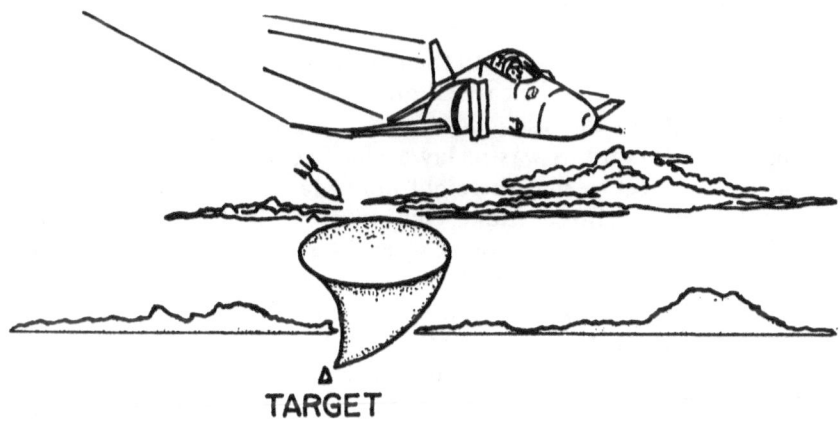

Laser Basket (Drawing).

fighter wing operating in North Vietnam. The wing, commanded at this time by Colonel (now Brig. General) Carl S. Miller, was soon to earn the title of "Bridge Busters" as a consequence of the wing's use of the new weapons against the North Vietnamese supply system. Between 6 April 1972 and 30 June 1972, the 8th TFW F-4 aircraft were to destroy a total of 106 bridges, including the Paul Doumer and the Thanh Hoa, with the new guided bombs.

In addition to the guided bombs, US air power had increased its capabilities by improving its electronic counter measures (ECM) through the use of "chaff" dropped from F-4 aircraft. "Chaff" is millions of small thin strips of an aluminum-like-substance cut in varying lengths, which are dropped by aircraft at high altitudes. The chaff causes a great deal of interference on radar scopes, which prevents the enemy form accurately identifying formations of aircraft and thereby degrades the radar's capability. This makes the operation of SAMs and radar-controlled AAA very difficult. The chaff was scattered by a flight of F-4 aircraft, several minutes ahead of the strike group, to provide a "chaff corridor" of specified length and width through which the attacking aircraft would fly. The use of chaff during Linebacker I operations was a significant factor in keeping aircraft losses low. (Linebacker I was the code name for the early 1972 air operations aimed at destroying North Vietnam's logistics system.)

Operation Freedom Dawn

With the authorization to reinitiate the bombing of North Vietnam, several air operations plans were drawn up to satisfy the interdiction requirements directed by the upper echelon planners. One of these plans, Freedom Dawn, included, among other targets, the Thanh Hoa Bridge. The plan called for a small tactical strike force to destroy the Dragon's Jaw with the new family of guided bombs.

The operation was to be carried out by 12 F-4 Phantoms from the 8th TFW, eight of them loaded with 2,000-pound guided weapons. A flight of 4 Phantoms was to lay a chaff corridor from the initial point to the target so that the eight bomb-laden F-4s could operate in a relatively sterilized radar environment. Bad weather in the target area had been the cause of several last minute postponements of the mission, but on 27 April 1972, reports indicated the weather had cleared sufficiently over Thanh Hoa to permit the strike.

On that day, the 12 Phantoms took off from Ubon, and the three flights of four aircraft each headed for an air refueling area where SAC KC-135 tankers were orbiting, waiting to off-load extra fuel to the fighters. This fuel might be necessary should enemy fighters appear or should the capping of a downed aircrew become a reality.

Having some extra JP-4 fuel might mean the difference between making one last turn to destroy an enemy MIG or being able to orbit a downed crewman and provide suppressive fire against ground forces until SAR aircraft arrived.

With several thousand pounds of fuel obtained from the tankers, the fighters headed for the bridge. The chaff delivery aircraft had gone out in front to form the protective cooridor in advance of the strike aircraft. However, as the strike aircraft approached the IP, a glance in the direction of the target revealed heavy cloud cover which could hamper the use of the guided bombs. The heavy cloud cover and poor visibility precluded the use of LGB illuminators to designate the target continuously. It was a day for the EOGB weapons. The aircraft carrying the EOGBs then positioned themselves for the strike, and let loose with five EOGBs. The extremely heavy anti-air-craft fire filled the skies with hundreds of white, gray and black puffs of smoke from exploding AAA shells. A number of SA-2 SAMs were fired at the aircraft, but SAM effectiveness was reduced by the chaff—so much so that the Phantoms excaped without a scratch. Post-mission photo reconnaissance showed the damage to the bridge to be entensive enough to render it unusable to vehicle traffic. The EOGBs had severely shaken the structure, but stubborn to the end, the Dragon's Jaw would need one more punch.

The Dragon Goes Down

On the 10th of May, Operation Linebacker I was initiated, the start of the increased interdiction effort in the north. Heavy air strikes were flown against targets in the Hanoi-Haiphong area and reduced to rubble many key objectives previously "off limits."

After three days of Linebacker activity, the Thanh Hoa Bridge once again was highlighted on the daily mission orders. The mission was to be similar to that flown on April 27th except the weather was forecast to be better and two additional aircraft were scheduled, making a total of 14 strike aircraft. Guided bombs were on the agenda again; however, this time, nine 3,000-pound LGBs would be used in conjuction with fifteen 2,000-pound LGBs and forty-eight 500-pound conventional bombs.

On the morning of 13 May, the attacking force members annotated their maps with updated SAM plots and received final briefings on enemy AAA defenses, air-refueling tracks, positions of supporting ECM forces and the SAR procedures. The target weather was briefed as good. The strike group took off on schedule and rendozvoused with the KC-135 tankers for the pre-strike refueling.

The pilots then set an easterly course across southern North Vietnam to the Gulf of Tonkin, and from there north to the target area. Approaching the target, everyone could see that the weather forecaster had been correct. No trouble — some clouds were evident and the flights positioned for the attack.

With the target in sight, the lead aircraft rolled in for the kill, unleashing his LGBs at the bridge. Plane after plane followed, with each pilot hoping that the anti-aircraft flashes on the ground did not signal a shot destined for his aircraft. As they dropped more bombs on the target, the last few pilots saw large clouds of dust spewing and belches of fire as the bombs exploded on the bridge. After the final aircraft had pulled away from the target, the strike pilots knew the bridge was down. The pilots headed for home — mission accomplished.

No aircraft had been damaged, even though the AAA and SAM fire had been intense. Post-strike photography by RF-4Cs confirmed the strike pilots' assessment. The western span of the bridge had been knocked completely off its 40 foot thick concrete abutment and the bridge superstructure was so critically disfigured and twisted that rail traffic would come to a standstill for at least several months.

The interdiction campaign against North Vietnam grew in intensity during May 1972, and the enemy LOCs showed signs of crumbling under the continuous assault by American air power. Guided bombs were used with increasing regularity and success.

By the end of May 1972, there were 13 important rail bridges down along the two major rail lines running northeast and northwest from Hanoi. There were another four rail bridges down between Hanoi and Haiphong, and several more had been dropped on the rail line running south from Hanoi.

Strikes Continue Against the Thanh Hoa Bridge

Although the bridge had been severely damaged on the 13 May strike, the ambitious North Vietnamese began immediately to repair the bridge so that rail traffic could again cross the Song Ma River. As a result, it was necessary to schedule strikes periodically to hinder the repair efforts. The Navy flew 11 more missions against the Thanh Hoa Bridge and the US Air Force two more missions before the 23rd of October 1972, the day President Nixon stopped all bombing of North Vietnam. With this bombing halt, the saga of the Dragon's Jaw come to a close. Although bombing would be seen over North Vietnam again during Linebacker II in December 1972, the Thanh Hoa bridge was not on the target list during the campaign, for it was still in a state of disrepair.

USAF F-4s dropping the western span of Thanh Hoa Bridge on 13 May 1972.

Doumer's Demise

The precision guided bombs that caused the destruction of the Thanh Hoa bridge also played a decisive role against the Paul Doumer bridge. Although this bridge did not have the same reputation as the Thanh Hoa, planners nevertheless knew that it would take a major US effort to destroy the Doumer and other key targets in the north. When the Linebacker I operation began on May 10, 1972, the 8 TFW was ordered to launch a large and carefully coordinated attack against the Yen Bien railroad marshalling yards and the Paul Doumer bridge. This was the first strike on the Doumer since 1967. The force composition included an armada of aircraft from other bases in Thailand to support the primary strike birds, reminiscent of earlier Rolling Thunder missions. The 8 TFW was tasked to supply the bombing punch with sixteen conventionally loaded F-4s and eight F-4s to provide chaff support. The 388 TFW at Korat would provide fifteen F-105G Wild Weasel aircraft for SAM suppression and four EB-66s for ECM support. As usual, MIG CAP would be supplied by Phantoms flying high in the target area.

On the morning of 10 May, with all mission planning complete, aircrews were briefed and the aircraft were loaded with MK-84 2,000-pound guided bombs. Although Linebacker had started at the onset of the southwest monsoon season, the weather appeared to be suitable and the decision was made to go.

The first aircraft off were the two flights of chaff-support F-4s at approximately 0800 hours. Approximately twenty minutes later, the strike aircraft lifted off the Ubon runway. The sixteen F-4s were launched in flights of four — "Jingle," "Napkin" and "Biloxi" flights were armed with LGBs while "Goatee" flight carried the EOGBs.

After refueling and flying deep into enemy territory, the strike flights located the chaff corridor on radar. The chaff birds had done their job well, laying down a protective corridor that would shield the strike aircraft during their final run to the target. The strike aircraft flew within this protective cover until the Doumer bridge came into view. Captain Mike Messett, leader of a 2-ship element on this mission, has vivid memories about the Doumer bridge. He was on the original strike in August 1967, and recalls that day in particular because he was hit by AAA shortly after rolling-in on the target. He was a "back-seater" in those days, and the AAA exploded through the front canopy and disabled the aircraft commander. Captain Messett recovered the aircraft, released ordnance, and "got the hell out of Dodge." Recovery was complex and entailed emergency in-flight refueling and a rear seat landing back at Ubon. He was subsequently awarded the Silver Star for that trip to Mr. Doumer's bridge and, as Captain Messett said, "I had a long unsettled grudge against that bridge."

Captain Messett got his chance on May 10. As his flight reached the desired altitude and roll-in point, the wingmen moved in to within 4 shipwidths of each other. The element moved well forward since the final turn for roll-in was away from them. All aircraft had to maintain this integrity during the entire maneuver in order for the bombs to enter the LGB "basket" that the flight lead would create.

Captain Messett was monitoring the progress of the preceding elements as best he could to get a feel for possible variations in the

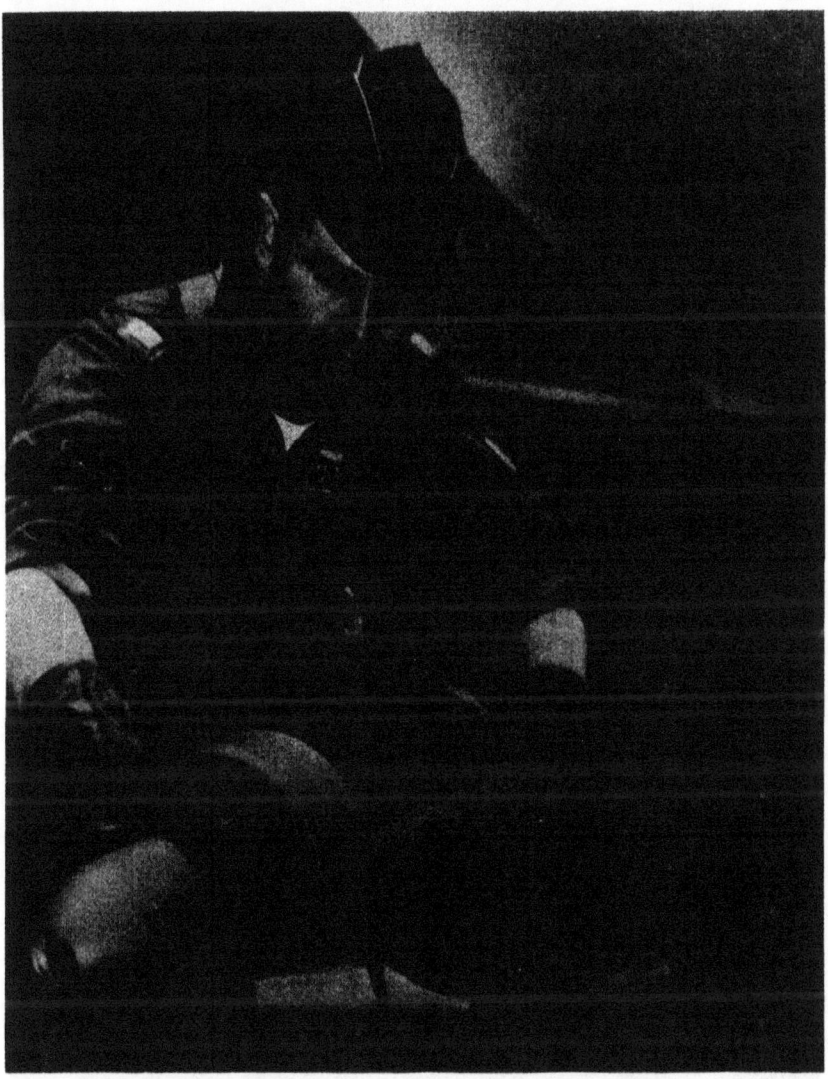

Capt Thomas "Mike" Messett is shown checking a 2,000 pound Laser Guided Bomb loaded on his F-4E before a strike mission "up north." Capt Messett participated in three strikes on the Doumer Bridge.

pre-briefed plan. He saw several bombs impact on the superstructure, but many of the bombs hadn't hit yet. His flight leader released his bombs at about 14,000 feet and that was his visual cue to release. The flak in the area was heavy, but as Captain Messett said, "So what." Although it was difficult to observe spans drop, he was convinced the bridge took many hits.

All flights encountered heavy AAA ground fire and it was later estimated that more than 160 SAMs were fired at the strike force that day. Add the 41 MIGs that were launched and it is obvious that the North Vietnam skies were a very unfriendly place to be on that day in May 1972. It seems hard to believe that not a single aircraft was lost in the assault on the Doumer bridge. A great deal of credit for this remarkable record went to the support crews whose job it was to protect the strike force — Wild Weasels, chaff aircraft, ECM birds and the F-4 MIG CAP.

The bombing results achieved were excellent. A total of 22 LGB and seven EOGB 2,000-pounders were expended by the force. After returning to Ubon from the three-hour mission, aircrews reported that 12 bombs had scored direct hits, four were probables and 13 could not be observed due to smoke and enemy defenses. The reconnaissance photos showed conclusively that the bridge had been rendered unusable. Several spans were damaged and one span was destroyed, effectively stopping rail traffic from the north to Hanoi. When asked to report on the bridge damage, one flight leader stated simply "one severely smoking bridge."

The mission was a success, and the Ubon Officers Club was packed that afternoon as war stories were told and re-told. Captain Messett

An F-4 dropping a MK-84 Laser Guided Bomb.

said it was tremendous to see the Doumer again and it was absolutely exhilarating to get his "sweet revenge." Little did Captain Messett know that he would make one more trip to Mr. Doumer's bridge.

To make sure that the bridge stayed down, a follow-up raid was planned for the next day. Convinced now that the guided bombs had deadly effectiveness, only four aircraft were fragged to reattack the bridge. One of these aircraft would be carrying two of the impressive M118, 3,000-pound bombs. This was the bomb that dropped the Doumer in 1967. These bombs, if delivered on target, would put the finishing touch on the bridge.

On the afternoon of 11 May, a flight of four F-4s from the 8 TFW carried out the second raid. Captain Messett and his roommate, Captain Dave Smith, were both scheduled to lead flights up north that day, but Captain Messett drew the Doumer Bridge. To their complete amazement, they were to be the only strike forces in Route Pack Six that afternoon. Captain Smith was scheduled to strike the Bac Mai Command Post just inside the southern city limits of Hanoi.

Everything was normal and no problem encountered as both flights proceeded inbound to their targets using the same route as the day before. Then came the realization that the chaff had been dropped too early due to a mix-up on target times, and the MIG CAP and support flights had left early thinking the strike flight were not coming. No MIGs harrassed either flight, but they did receive significant attention from the SAMs. Because they were such a small force, Captain Messett was concerned that the SAM sites would have an easy day working them over. As he passed his roommate who was busy with his target, a few SAMs got very close to him and some actually went through the flight but failed to detonate.

It was at least another two minutes until he crossed Hanoi to set up on the east side for roll-in. Oddly enough, the SAMs ceased and the AAA was not in evidence. As Captain Messett said, "I think the North Vietnamese couldn't believe what was going on." Target acquistion was simple with no other aircraft to watch, and he observed at least one span in the water with an adjacent one heavily damaged. He elected to pick a span near the Hanoi side because of his position. Release and tracking went excellently, and the GIB (Guy-in-backseat) observed multiple impacts on the causeway. Although it's impossible to see a span drop while on the bomb run, the observed direct hits gave a favorable probability. Captain Messett was hoping it was "rush hour."

The egress was quite smooth—almost eerie because no defenses of any sort harassed the flight. Captain Messett was elated, knowing that his flight of four had done as much damage as the entire strike force the day before.

A total of eight LBGs was expended, including the two M118s and six MK84, 2,000-pounders and the results were phenomenal! Three additional spans had been dropped into the river, and three other spans significantly damaged. The Paul Doumer would not be a target for some months to come.

Unfavorable weather during much of the next few months precluded any further attacks against the Doumer bridge. However, the significant damage inflicted on 10 to 11 May proved sufficient to keep the bridge out of commission for a long time. This was confirmed on 10 September, when the weather cleared enough for a flight of four F-4s and the 8 TFW to strike the bridge "one more time." This attack successfully dropped two more spans and the damage report showed that the enemy had not yet been able to reuse the bridge.

By 13 May, both the Paul Doumer and Thanh Hoa bridge were down — a tribute to all of the airmen who had bravely participated in these missions throughout the long years of the Vietnam war. A significant factor in this success story was phenomenal accuracy achieved with guided bombs. With fewer strike aircraft required to assure target destruction, more targets could be attacked and a larger number of aircraft assigned to defending the strike force. The higher bomb release altitudes helped keep the fighters our of the deadly AAA range, thereby lowering loss rates significantly.

With the help of technology and training, airmen with determination, courage and professional skill finally were able to bring the "Tale of Two Bridges" to a convincing close. Their story is but one of many in the long Vietnam experience where airpower was applied and the report came back. . . .

"Mission accomplished!"

Thanh Hoa Bridge as it appeared following a successful strike by F–4s on 13 May 1972.

The Thanh Hoa RR and highway bridge 2½ miles north northeast of Thanh Hoa following its collapse under direct bomb hits by USS America carrier pilots on 6 Oct 1972.

Photo showing the conclusive results of the F–4 attacks on the Doumer Bridge on 10–11 May 1972.

Post-strike photo showing the destroyed spans of the Doumer Bridge after the 10 Sep 1972 strike by F-4s from the 8th Tactical Fighter Wing.

MONOGRAPH 2

The Battle for the Skies Over North Vietnam
1964-1972

Authors: Major Paul Burbage
Major Eli Gateff
Major James Hoffman
Major Blaine Lotz
Major Addison Rawlins
Major Barry Swarts
Major Ron Walker
Major Rudolph Zuberbuhler

Monograph Edited by

Lt Colonel Gordon Nelson
Major Norm Wood

Authors' Acknowledgements

The facilities at Maxwell AFB offer a rich variety of source materials for the study of airpower in Southeast Asia. We are grateful to Mr. Robert B. Lane and his staff of the Air University Library, Lt Col Malcom S. Bounds of the Maxwell Corona Harvest office, and Mr. Lloyd H. Cornett, Jr., and his staff at the Albert F. Simpson Historical Research Center.

We are indebted to the staff of the *AU Review* who reviewed the manuscripts and provided valuable editing assistance.

Additionally, we are indebted to the many Air University personnel who provided support and assistance throughout the project.

Finally, we are deeply indebted to the Office of Air Force History (AF/CHO) and to the Directorate of Doctrine, Concepts and Objectives (AF/XOD), Headquarters, USAF for their assistance in the final editing and publication. We are particularly grateful to Major Charles N. Wood from AF/XOD for his help in the initial editing process.

Table of Contents

Introduction	....	103
Chapter I.	PRELUDE TO A SHOWDOWN	107
	Factors Affecting Aerial Operations	108
Chapter II.	EARLY USE OF AIRPOWER	112
	The Opposition: North Vietnamese Fighter Buildup	112
	U.S. Air Superiority Capabilities	113
	Quality of U.S. Aircrews	120
	Early Lessons Learned	120
Chapter III.	ROLLING THUNDER (MARCH 1965 – DECEMBER 1965)	125
	The Bombing Begins in Earnest	125
	The First MIG Attacks	126
	The First MIG Kills	127
	SAMs and More MIGs	130
Chapter IV.	AIR SUPERIORITY COMES OF AGE	134
	Status of Rival Capabilities	134
	Rolling Thunder Resumes	135
	MIGs and Operation Bolo	139
	Moves and Countermoves	145
Chapter V.	BOMBING OF THE NORTH RESUMES: OPERATION LINEBACKER I	147
	Policy and Other Changes	149
	Air Superiority Enters a New Phase	151
	Technology Versus Enemy Defenses	157
	Oyster Flight on a Linebacker Mission ...	159
	A Hunter-Killer Mission Against Combined Air Defenses	165
	Sowing Protective Corridors	167
	Reflections on Linebacker I	173
Chapter VI.	LINEBACKER II AND THE END OF HOSTILITIES	175
	Peace Negotiations	175
	The Big Push	175
	Planning Considerations	176
	Building a Strike Force	176
	The First Three Days	177
	The Tactics Change	184
	The Post-Christmas Operations	185
	The Final Thrust	187

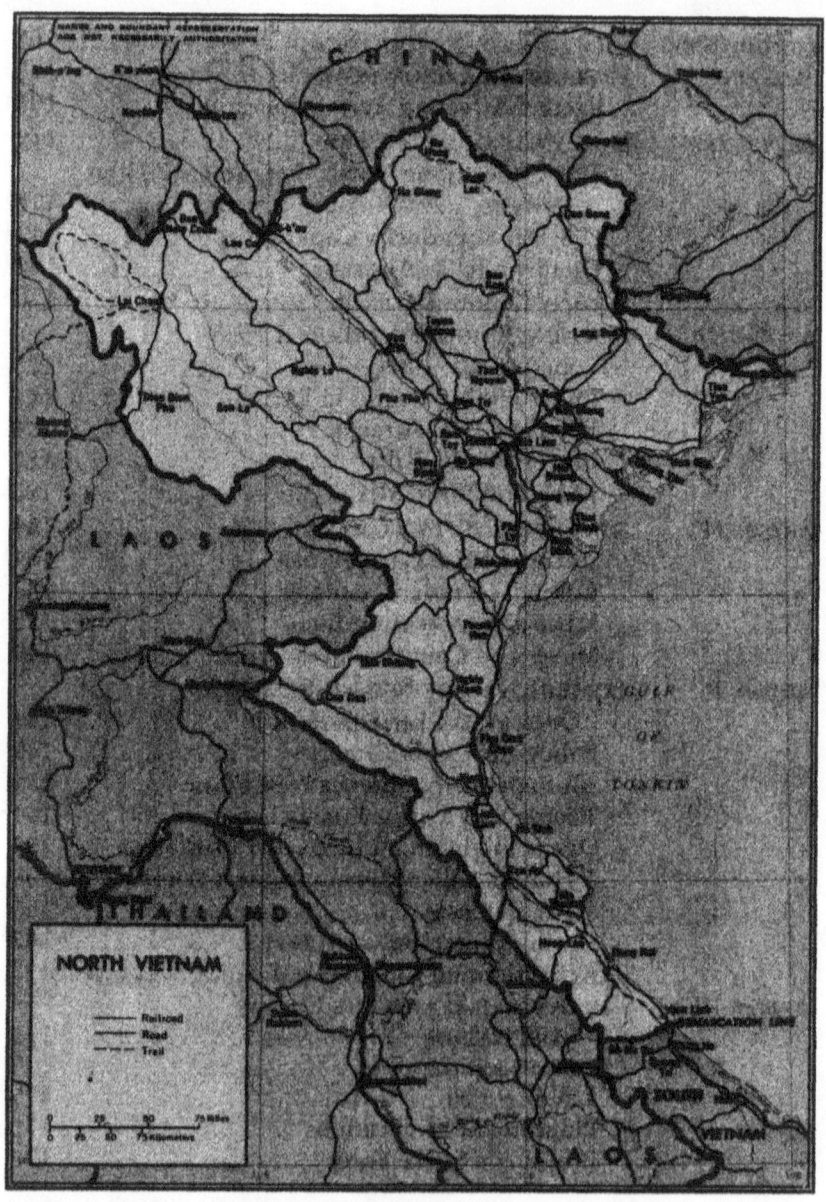

Introduction

This is the story of US air superiority over North Vietnam (NVN). It begins with the first US air strikes in 1964 and runs for eight long years of gradually increasing applications of airpower — "gradualism" it was called. It ends with the superbly planned and executed air activity known as Linebacker II in December 1972.

Linebacker II achieved in a few short days absolute US air supremacy. When the Air Force completed this operation, B-52s, F-4s, F-105s, F-111s, A-7s, rescue helicopters, and all the associated support aircraft roamed the skies of North Vietnam at will.

No longer were MIGs and surface-to-air missiles (SAMs) able to threaten US aircrews or add to the number of prisoners of war held by Hanoi. Only an anti-aircraft artillery threat was left to harass the airmen.

Many courageous airmen gave their lives fighting through the hostile skies of North Vietnam. Many more dedicated years of training, planning, and hard work to US efforts. There were jubilant victories and crushing setbacks. Political and diplomatic considerations necessitated restraints in the application of air power — to some airmen, it seemed that this prevented them from "winning" the war in the traditional military sense.

Within this context the Air Force worked long and hard to maintain air superiority. Restrained from attacking some politically sensitive targets, airmen fought through the same ground and air defenses daily in order to "go North," to destroy and restrict the supplies feeding the war in the South.

This monograph depicts the evolution of US aerial tactics over North Vietnam. It describes how airmen, although [restricted] in the application of air power, still managed to accomplish their tasks. It is part of the story of the Air Force at war over North Vietnam.

This monograph was researched and written by a team of men who trained for and/or fought in that war; men who saw many varying aspects of that war. While assembled as students at the Air Command and Staff College, Maxwell Air Force Base, Alabama, the following officers joined to reconstruct the events in this history.

>   Major Paul Burbage
>   Major Eli Gateff
>   Major James Hoffman
>   Major Blaine Lotz
>   Major Addison Rawlins
>   Major Barry Swarts
>   Major Ron Walker
>   Major Rudolph Zuberhuhler

They were assisted by their faculty leader and editor, Colonel Lloyd Houchin, and a faculty reader, Lieutenant Colonel Gordon Nelson.

Major Burbage is the only monograph team member without experience in Southeast Asia (SEA). An F-4 pilot with extensive knowledge of air-to-air combat tactics, Major Burbage participated in two F-4 squadron deployments to Korea in response to US commitments there. He was an instructor in air superiority tactics for two years.

Major Eli Gateff flew 29 missions over North Vietnam during five temporary duty tours as a radar navigator in the B-52D. He flew a total of 254 combat missions during the period form September 1969 to December 1972. He participated in both Linebacker I and Linebacker II strike operations.

Major James Hoffman's operational experience includes 89 missions over North Vietnam during 1968 while he was assigned to the 433d Tactical Fighter Squadron, Ubon RTAFB, Thailand, as an F-4 weapon systems officer.

Major Lotz served in Vietnam during 1967-1968 as an intelligence watch officer assigned to the Headquarters, Seventh Air Force Warning Center, Tan Son Nhut Air Base, South Vietnam. His assignment spanned the North Vietnamese Tet and May offensives of 1968. Following his Vietnam tour, Major Lotz worked at Headquarters, Pacific Air Force on an intelligence study of the air war in North Vietnam. He was then assigned to the Air Staff Combat Application Group, Headquarters USAF, where he continued to work in Southeast Asian affairs.

Major "Ace" Rawlins flew 116 missions in SEA of which 100 were over NVN in 1966-67. Assigned to the 8th Tactical Fighter Wing (TFW) and flying the F-104C from Udorn RTAFB, Thailand, he participated in a variety of missions including interdiction, escort, and combat air patrol (CAP), and in Operation Bolo, an effective counter air operation that destroyed seven airborne MIGs in one day.

Major Swarts was an F-105 strike pilot stationed at Korat RTAFB during 1968-1969. He flew 29 missions over NVN prior to the bombing halt of 1 November 1968. He spent the last months of his tour at

Seventh Air Force Headquarters where he monitored the combat test and evaluation of new weapons entering the SEA theater.

Major Walker participated in attacks against North Vietnam during two major campaigns. As a strike pilot in the F-105, he flew 48 missions over NVN before the bombing halt ended the Rolling Thunder effort in 1968. Returning again to Takhli RTAFB in September 1972, he logged an additional 27 NVN missions in the F-111, many of which were in the Hanoi area in support of Linebacker II.

Major Rudolph Zuberbuhler flew 300 combat missions of which 146 were over North Vietnam. These missions were flown during 1965, 1966, and 1972 from Ubon RTAFB, Thailand. He participated in Linebacker I as a flight commander in an F-4 squadron. On 12 September 1972, his aircraft was shot down over North Vietnam and he became a prisoner of war. He was released on 29 March 1973.

Colonel Houchin's Vietnam experience spans seven years of the war. Involved in the first jet fighter activities there in 1964, he was back again in 1965. Flying F-100s, on both temporary duty tours, he flew 56 missions over North Vietnam. During 1970-71, he was an advisor to a Vietnamese Air Force wing commander.

Lieutenant Colonel Gordon Nelson flew 135 missions over North Vietnam in the B-57. Approximately 60 percent of these missions were flown at night. Between 1965 and 1972 he was an instructor pilot instructing fighter tactics. In 1973-74 he was chief of the weapons and tactics branch at Udorn RTAFB.

These officers flew an aggregate total of 632 missions over North Vietnam against MIGs, SAMs, and AAA. This is their story of the evolution of American air superiority over the North. They were there.

Chapter I.   Prelude to a Showdown

Captain Steve Ritchie from Reidsville, North Carolina, was leading a flight of F-4 "Phantoms". His four aircraft were protecting a strike force as it departed a target near Hanoi, and headed for Udorn Royal Thai Air Force Base (RTAFB), Thailand. EC-121 radar support aircraft offshore warned the F-4 crews that MIGs were aloft. The information, however, was too late to help the F-4s carrying chaff dispensers. Enemy radar had vectored a MIG-21 pilot in behind the chaff aircraft.[1] he rapidly moved in, fired an ATOLL heat seeking missile and broke away to safety.

The ATOLL hit the left engine of one of the chaff escorts. With a badly crippled F-4, the pilot headed out of the target area while transmitting his position, heading, and altitude on the radio guard channel. Meanwhile another pilot in a fighter flying cover against MIGs for the benefit of strike forces (MIGCAP) had to depart too, because his plane had an engine fire.

Captain Ritchie, knowing that North Vietnamese ground radar controllers would direct their MIGs against crippled aircraft, descended to a lower altitude, about 5,000 feet above ground. Learning from Navy radar and the orbiting Air Force EC-121 that two MIGs were two miles north of the flight, Captain Ritchie turned north to intercept the MIGs.

Within seconds he made visual contact with the lead aircraft — close enough to see a silver MIG-21 with bright red star markings. Recalling that a common NVN tactic was to send a single MIG out front as a decoy, Captain Ritchie refused the baited trap, rolled his aircraft and dove closer to the ground. Soon he saw the second MIG pass overhead approximately 10,000 feet behind the first. The ploy of the MIG pilots had failed; now they were the hunted.

Captain Ritchie began a hard slicing 6½ G turn to get into position behind the second MIG fighter. He had the MIG in his gun sight and the radar was locked on, providing range information. After several seconds he squeezed the trigger twice, firing two Sparrow radar mis-

---

[1] An aircraft that dispenses narrow metallic strips used to reflect echoes for radar confusion purposes.

siles. The first missile exploded in the center of the MIG fuselage; the second missile went through the fireball.

Usually when MIG pilots worked in pairs, the remaining pilot fled when his companion experienced trouble. However in this case, the red-starred MIG leader stayed in the fight and tried to shoot down the number four aircraft in Captain Ritchie's flight.

In response to the number four crew's request for assistance, Captain Ritchie descended to gain speed and made another hard turn just in time to get into firing position as the MIG pilot was maneuvering to destroy the number four aircraft. But the MIG pilot sensed his danger and initiated a hard turn back into his attacker. There was time for just the one missile to come off Ritchie's F-4. It shot straight out, made a near 90 degree turn, and smashed dead center into the fuselage of the MIG-21. The enemy aircraft disintegrated in a huge fireball.

Factors Affecting Aerial Operations

The Fighter pilots have to rove in the area allotted to them in any way they like, and when they spot an enemy they attack and shoot him down; anything else is rubbish.

— Baron Von Richthofen
World War I

Captain Ritchie's victories over North Vietnam confirmed that Von Richthofen's quotation was still valid, even though closure speeds had increased ten-fold. Since the first air combat, in Von Richthofen's day, pilots have known the importance of sighting the enemy early. World War II airspeeds increased the problem, but not until the Korean conflict and the birth of the jet age did "spotting the enemy" become a foremost problem. By the start of the Vietnam war, closure rates in excess of 1,000 knots were common.

Even though Captain Ritchie was successful, many of his fellow airmen lost the tactical advantage because they still had to visually identify the enemy prior to attacking. What was needed was a better way of separating friend from foe. By the end of the Vietnam war, technology had provided a better mousetrap. But, in the beginning we were fighting at jet age speeds using horse and buggy tactics.

There are however, more subtle aspects to localized air superiority. Many conditions lend themselves to survival in an air-to-air encounter. Pilots cite the ability to use surprise and judgment — namely, the ability to size up situations quickly and accurately and to take advantage of them. In North Vietnam, most US aircraft shot down by MIGs were the result of enemy pilots achieving surprise over their US counterparts. The element of surprise was critical. The fighter pilot

The MIG Killers (11 Aug 1972) Front row: Capt Charles Debellevue (6 MIGs) and Capt Richard S. Ritchie (5 MIGs) Back row: Lt Col Griff Baily (2 MIGs) and Capt Jeff Feinstein (5 MIGs).

who could not react automatically and correctly to an array of dangers probably did not make the kill—or worse yet, got shot down himself.

Some of these factors worked for Captain Ritchie and his flight of F-4s; factors such as preparation, teamwork, and discipline. But the enemy had some advantages also. The North Vietnamese had a highly sophisticated ground controlled radar environment. The MIG-21 was about half the size of the F-4 and left very little smoke; the F-4 left two large smoke trails that made it much easier to see. The MIG-21 turned tighter, a very important attribute which counteracted the better speed and acceleration of the F-4. The MIGs were specifically designed for air superiority, while the US aircraft involved in North Vietnam were not. During the Cold War period following World War II, the US built fighters to perform multiple missions rather than single missions such as air superiority and another for tactical bombardment. The lighter and smaller MIGs were harder to see and they were able to turn in a smaller radius. The F-4, on the other hand, had greater acceleration and US aircraft, in general, had better armament. US pilots had to be able to cope with these differences; to exploit their aircraft's special capabilities to best advantage, and to avoid fighting when MIGs had the advantage.

Other factors affected the battle for air superiority. Anti-aircraft artillery (AAA) and automatic weapons could limit use of airspace closer to the ground. Surface-to-air missiles impinged upon USAF air superiority by forcing some aircraft to a lower altitude in order to avoid the SAMs. At the lower altitude, of course, aircraft were vulnerable to AAA and automatic weapons. Rules of engagement provided additional constraints. Decisions not to bomb airfields and key strategic installations, not to fire upon North Vietnamese aircraft unless attacked first, and not to attack unless visual contact was achieved all affected the tactics used to achieve air superiority.

In an overall sense, air superiority is not an all or nothing proposition. There are varying degrees of it. The highest degree of air superiority is called air supremacy. The US achieved air supremacy by the end of World War II against Germany and Japan. During the Korean War, the degree of US air superiority was indicated by the kill ratio of US fighter aircraft to those of North Korea: 12:1. In Southeast Asia, on the other hand, at the end of Rolling Thunder, the kill ratio was 2.5:1. In all cases, air superiority was reflected at one time or another in varying degrees.

Essentially, air superiority is achieved by the force that can deny the opposing force effective use of the air space while simultaneously accomplishing its particular mission. Yet, air superiority may be gained today and lost tomorrow. There were times that the US did not have local air superiority over North Vietnam. Thus, air superiority is required to decrease the ability of enemy aircraft and defenses to interfere with the operation of friendly forces. It follows that the first and highest priority task of tactical air forces in a theater of operations is to achieve air superiority. The Air Force has many missions to perform; but if air superiority is not established and maintained, then accomplishment of the others may not be possible.

Chapter II. Early Use of Airpower

By the end of May 1964, the JCS had made definitive proposals to use airpower against North Vietnam. The intent of attacking targets in North Vietnam had been to stop military aggression against South Vietnam. But, by August the focus of the war changed dramatically because NVN torpedo boats attacked US destroyers in the Gulf of Tonkin. These attacks set the stage for intensified use of airpower against North Vietnam.

The Opposition: North Vietnamese Fighter Buildup

Prior to the Tonkin incident, the North Vietnamese had no air defense fighter capability. They possessed only 30 trainer aircraft, 50 transports, and four light helicopters. On 7 August, two days after the Tonkin incident, the USAF identified MIG fighters that appeared at Phuc Yen Airfield near Hanoi. These were MIG-15s/17s provided by Communist China.

The size of the North Vietnamese Air Force remained unchanged until mid-June 1965 when additional MIG-15s and 17s from the Soviet Union brought the total to 70 fighter aircraft. It was more than a year after the Tonkin incident, in December 1965, before the North Vietnamese would receive the first MIG-21s, an aircraft comparable to the USAF's best air-to-air fighter.

The acquisition of the MIG-15s and 17s helped the North Vietnamese improve their air force. The two Soviet-designed subsonic fighters were both heavily armed. Each carried one 37mm and two 23mm cannons, and could carry rockets or bombs under the wings. The MIG-15 would prove relatively unimportant in the North Vietnam air war and claimed no known kills. However, this would not be the case for the MIG-17. These fighter aircraft were the first employed in North Vietnam as air defense forces.

In the early summer of 1964, the North Vietnamese had only two modern airfields capable of sustaining jet operations: Gia Lam Airfield at Hanoi and Cat Bi Airfield near Haiphong. Phuc Yen was un-

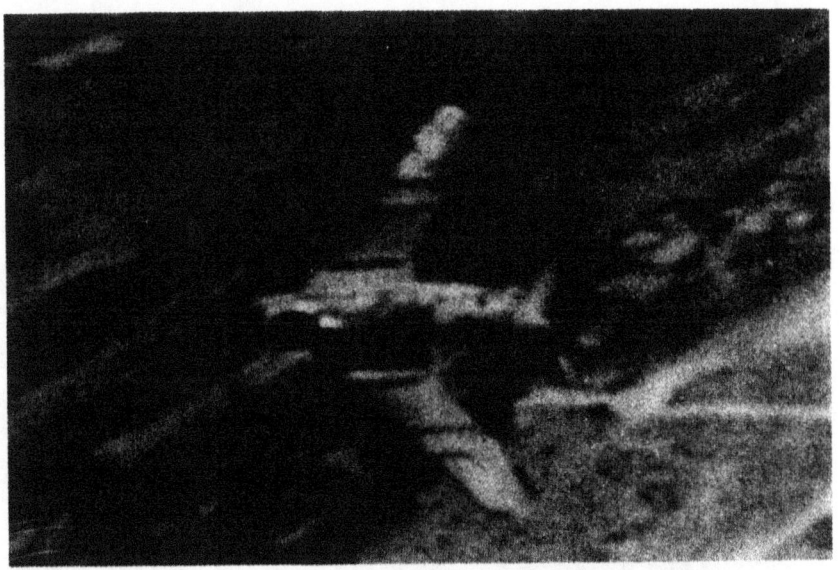

MIG-17 in dog fight with F-4, 1 May 1967.

der construction and nearing completion. By 7 August 1964 it received MIG-15s and 17s. Two other airfields, Kien An at Haiphong and Dong Hoi, just north of the Demilitarized Zone, had hard surface runways and were capable of supporting limited jet operations. Four additional airfields were built later, including Kep which was north of Hanoi, about one-third of the way to China. During most of the war, Phuc Yen and Kep remained the primary military airfields where the majority of aircraft were deployed. Gia Lam, Cat Bi, and Kien An were utilized as dispersal bases to provide for flexibility in the employment of fighters to protect key areas.

Other aspects of the North Vietnamese air defense system were very weak in 1964. The NVN forces possessed no surface-to-air missiles and conventional antiaircraft weapons numbered only about 700. The radar complex consisted of about 20 early warning radars, with very little definitive tracking capability. Overall, air defense was limited to key population areas and military installations and was mainly restricted to altitudes below 20,000 feet. This, then, was the picture of the North Vietnamese Air Force. By the end of 1964 they possessed only 34 fighter aircraft. These were MIG-15s and MIG-17s based at Phuc Yen.

US Air Superiority Capabilities

The friendly Southeast Asia air defense role was assigned to the Convair-designed F-102 all-weather interceptor. It was capable of supersonic flight and was armed with six air-to-air guided missiles

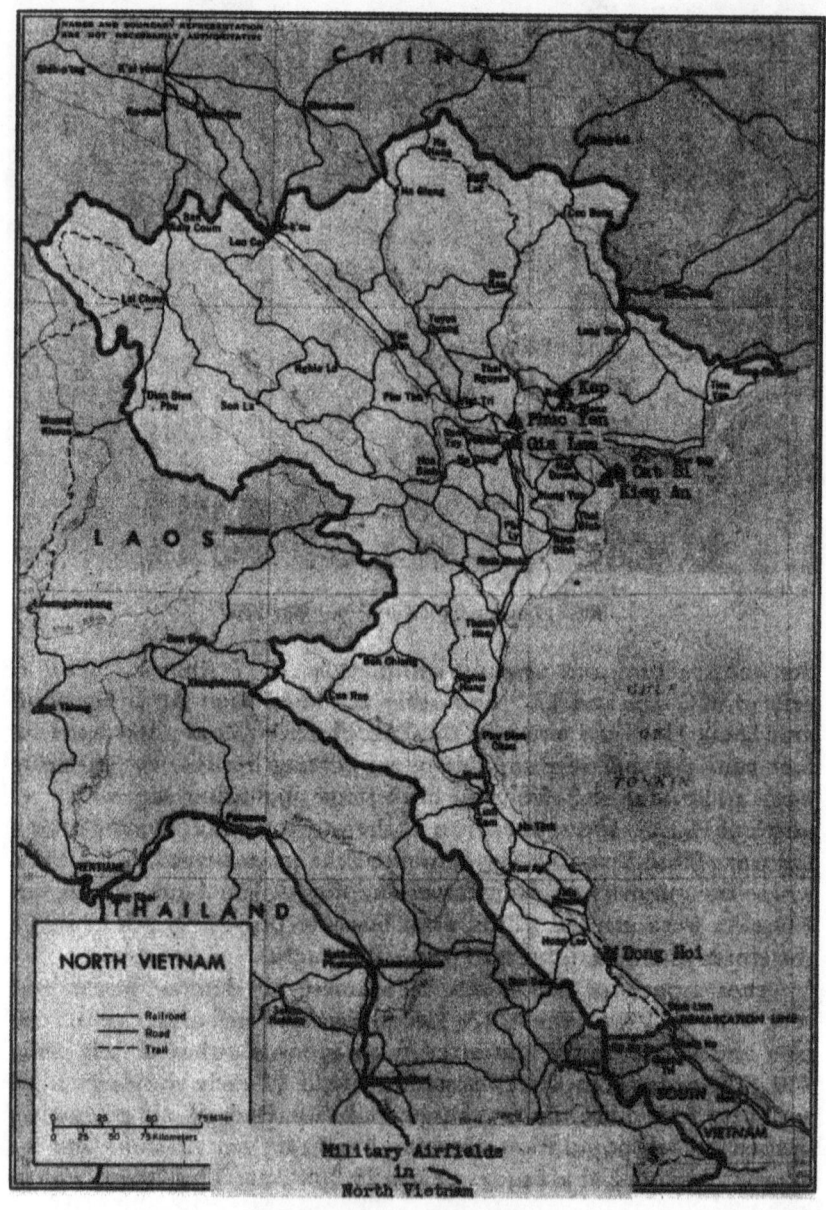

Military airfields in North Vietnam.

and twenty-four 2.75 inch diameter folding fin rockets. Though the F-102 would remain on active alert at bases in South Vietnam until 1968, it did not play a significant role over North Vietnam.

The F-100 Super Saber was given the role of fighter escort early in the war. It first flew in 1953 and was produced in several versions including the two seat "F" model. This aircraft was the first US fighter capable of supersonic speeds in level flight. The F-100's basic armament consisted of four 20mm cannons mounted in the nose; it could carry missiles and air-to-ground weapons under the wings. The "D" and "F" models used in Vietnam were in-flight refuelable and could carry external fuel tanks.

The most advanced US Air Force aircraft deployed into Southeast Asia during 1964 was the F-105 Thunderchief, built by Republic Aviation Corporation. Over 600 of these aircraft were built. Affectionately known as the "Thud," this aircraft was a single seat, all-weather fighter-bomber capable of speeds in excess of Mach 1 at sea level and over Mach 2.1 above 36,000 feet. It was equipped with sophisticated navigation equipment, and had radar capable of ground mapping as well as air search and tracking. It had an air refueling capability and could carry external fuel tanks. Internal armament included a 20mm, M-61 "Vulcan" multi-barrel cannon with 1,029 rounds of ammunition. The gun was capable of firing at rates of 6,000 rounds per minute. It could carry air-to-ground weapons in an internal bomb bay or under the wings and fuselage.

For the air-to-air mission, the "Thud" could carry the "Sidewinder" heat-seeking missiles under the wings. From 1964 through the end of the Southeast Asia war, the F-105 saw constant combat over the North. Compared to the MIG-17, it was faster, but it could not turn as tightly. This was due to the relative size and weight of the two aircraft. The F-105 was a large aircraft, approximately 69 feet long, with a short wing span of only 35 feet. Its empty weight totaled more than 28,000 pounds (F-105F), with a maximum takeoff weight of 54,000 pounds. In contrast, the MIG-17 had a wing span of 36 feet and weighed only 9,850 pounds empty; fully loaded it weighed 15,500 pounds. This resulted in a much reduced wing loading, or weight per square foot of wing area, thus giving it a much tighter turn capability.

By 1 December 1964, the F-100s and F-105s had been moved into South Vietnam at Da Nang and Bien Hoa to augment the forces already there. Other US forces were based throughout Southeast Asia. In Thailand, there were Ubon, Udorn, Korat, Takhli, Nakhon Phanom, and Don Muang Air Bases. In South Vietnam, there were Da Nang, Bien Hoa, Tan Son Nhut, Pleiku, and Nha Trang. As the war progressed most of the flights over the North were flown from only a few of these bases. The primary ones were Udorn, Takhli, Korat, Ubon, Da Nang, and Cam Ranh Bay after it became operational in mid-1965.

The air defense radar coverage was extended considerably in both Thailand and South Vietnam, with new radars that would be the principal sites throughout the war. Near Da Nang on "Monkey Mountain" was the "Panama" radar. At Pleiku, the "Peacock" radar

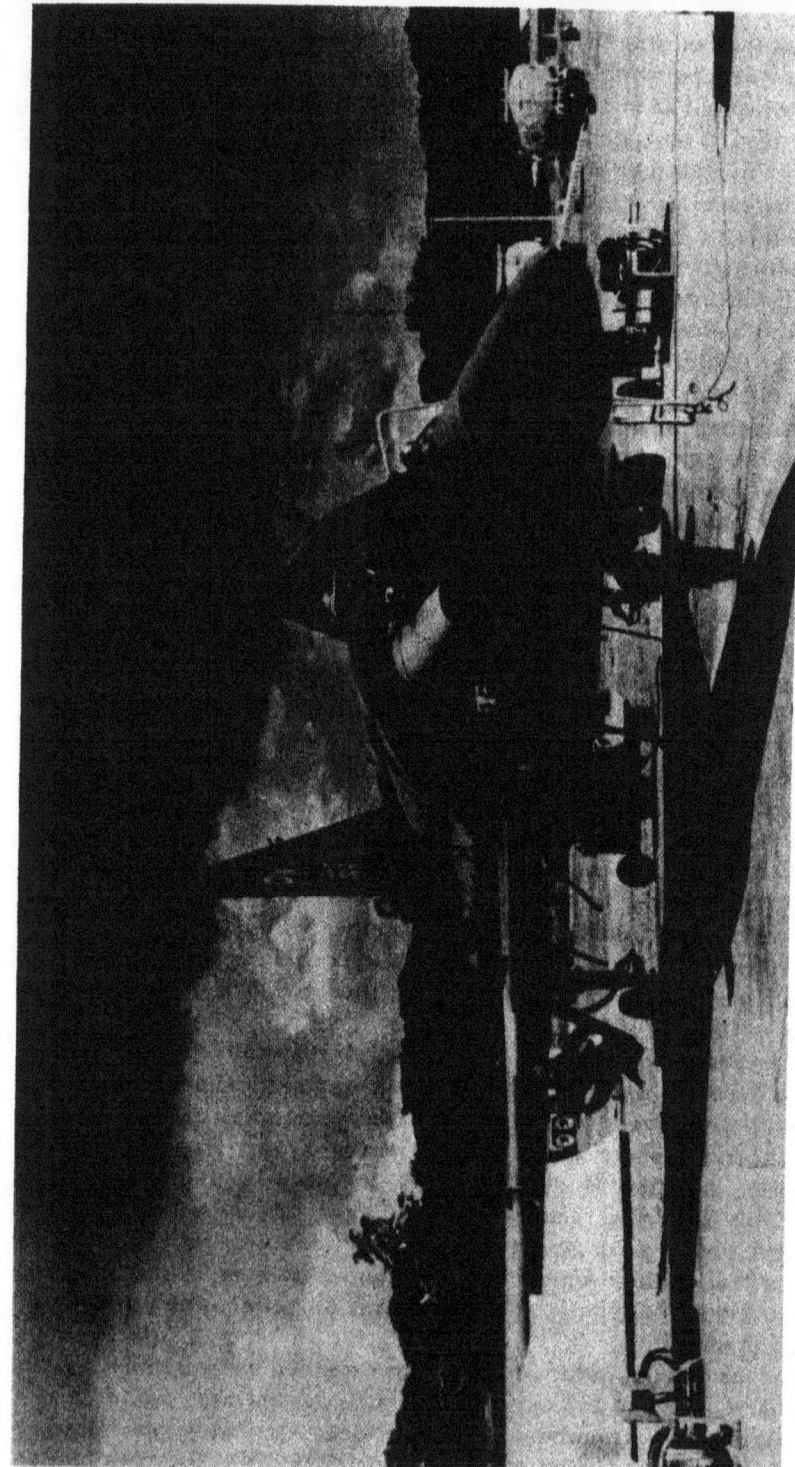

USAF F-102 at Udorn RTAFB, Thailand, 20 Sep 1968.

F-100 on a bombing mission, 1966.

F-105 "Thunderchief," armed with AGM-45 "SHRIKE" missiles, enroute to a target in North Vietnam.

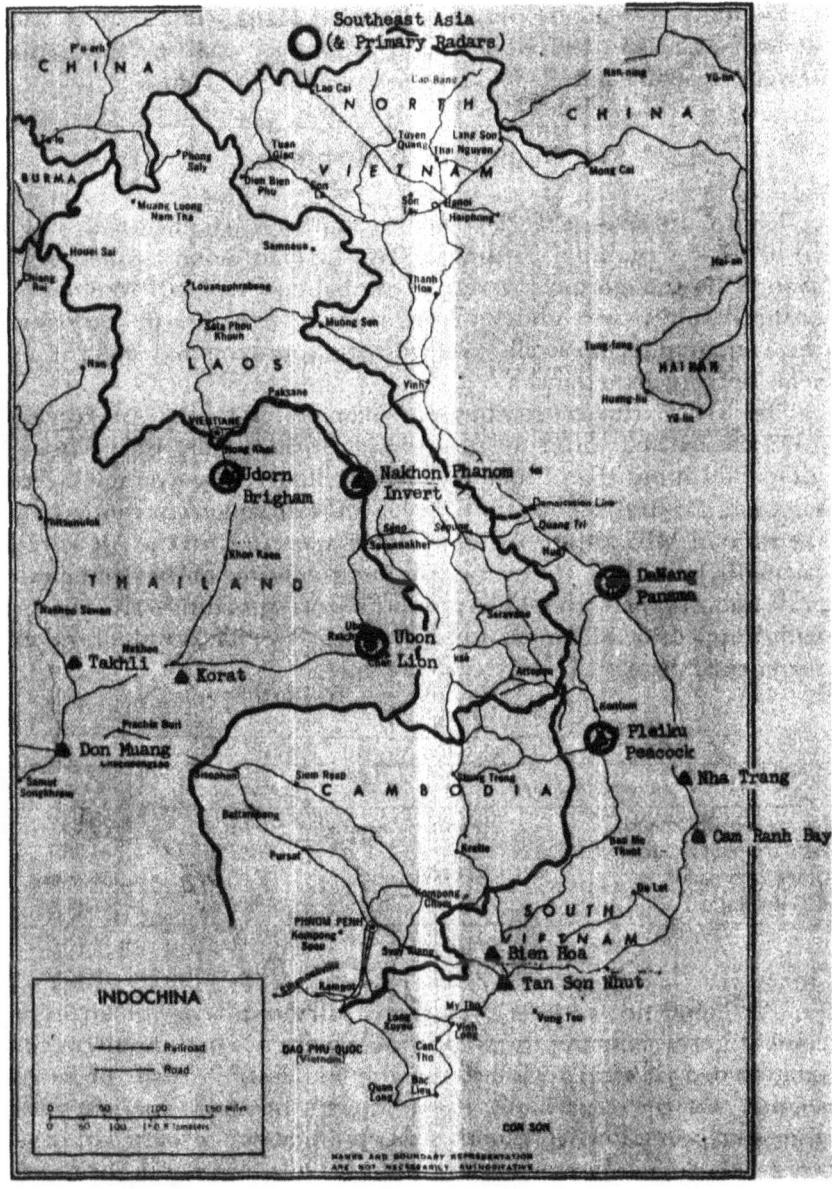

US Air Forces in Southeast Asia (& Primary Radars).

became operational. In Thailand, "Lion" was installed at Ubon RTAFB, "Brigham" at Udorn RTAFB, and "Invert" at Nakhon Phanom RTAFB. Fighter aircraft also deployed into the two countries to fulfill the air defense role. This was the picture of the friendly air defense forces.

By August 1964 there were F-100s at Da Nang and Takhli, F-102s at Da Nang, Tan Son Nhut, and Don Muang, and the Royal Australian Air Force had F-86Fs on alert at Ubon and Udorn.

Quality of US Aircrews

The US air forces that deployed to Southeast Asia in 1964 consisted of highly qualified personnel. The US had better trained pilots than NVN though most were not combat experienced. About 27% of the US pilots were under 30; nearly half were over 36; therefore, the average pilot was well-seasoned with approximately eight to ten years of flying experience.

The Red Baron air combat study conducted by the Air Force in 1973 showed that prior to June 1966 over 50 percent of the fighter pilots had more than 2,000 total flying hours; the average fighter pilot had flown 510 hours in the type aircraft he flew in combat and the ratio of MIG kills to Air Force losses was 3 to 1 in the Air Force's favor. By June 1968, the average fighter pilot time in the combat aircraft had dropped to 240 hours and the corresponding MIG kill rate had dropped to .85 for each of our losses. The background and experience of these pilots is portrayed below:

Command Experience	Apr 65-Jun 67	Jun 67-Mar 68
Tactical Air Command	64.5%	29.5%
Pilot Training Graduates	12.5%	21.1%
Other Commands	24.0%	49.4%
MIG Kill Ratio	3.0%	0.85%

Yet, one surprising fact surfaced in the analysis of air-to-air combat losses. Apparently total flying experience had no direct correlation to a US pilot's chances of being shot down in an air-to-air encounter. On the other hand, the pilot with the most experience had a greater probability of shooting down an enemy aircraft. In other words, experience counted in the offensive role, but not in the defensive role.

Early Lessons Learned

Generally, individual flight leaders determined their flight's combat tactics. Each flight was assigned a mission with a time on target (TOT), or a time period in the case of MIGCAP flights. The routes to and from the targets and the method of approaching the targets

F-86 Sabrejet of the Royal Australian Air Force at Don Muang Air Base, Thailand, June 1962.

were not specified; therefore, success depended upon how well individual flight leaders applied appropriate tactics.

One big factor that had to be considered throughout the war was the weather. Weather caused visual target sighting and navigation problems; but primarily it forced aircraft down into the range of AAA defenses. If the weather was very poor, an aircraft might even be within range of small arms fire the entire time the flight was over enemy territory.

Most of the antiaircraft weapons were Soviet made and their capabilities varied with size. The list below briefly describes each weapon.

Weapon	Most Lethal Range	Maximum Altitude
Quad 12.7mm	1000'	5,000'
Twin 14.5mm	1300'	6,500'
37mm	1400'	10,000'
57mm	1500-5000'	18,000'
85mm	5000-10,000'	25,000'
100mm	3000-20,000'	30,000'

Weapons of 57mm or larger could be radar controlled. These weapons are credited with shooting down 80 percent of the aircraft lost in 1965.

The lessons of the early operations were clear. Antiaircraft fire, not MIGs, was the main threat to US aircraft. To minimize losses, aircraft would have to avoid the AAA effective range envelope when possible or achieve surprise and complete attacks before AAA became active.

Avoiding effective AAA required pilots to approach the target at higher altitudes which resulted in earlier detection and, of course, loss of surprise. Moreover, as the targets became more heavily defended, defenses prevented most strafing attacks and aircraft were forced to remain above the most intense AAA while making only one bomb pass. Thus, bombing was less accurate, particularly when changing winds were a factor.

These first strikes into high threat areas started the development of new tactics and weapons to counter the air defense system. The perspective on defense of the aircraft was continually changing. It was driven by the threat. Higher altitudes escaped the AAA optimum ranges, but placed the aircraft in the envelope for SAM activation. Later in the war, when the MIGs were more numerous, the air-to-air threat compounded the defensive tactics. Flying too low meant AAA reaction; flying at medium altitudes meant SAM reaction—the MIG became a problem at all altitudes. This evolution continued throughout the war.

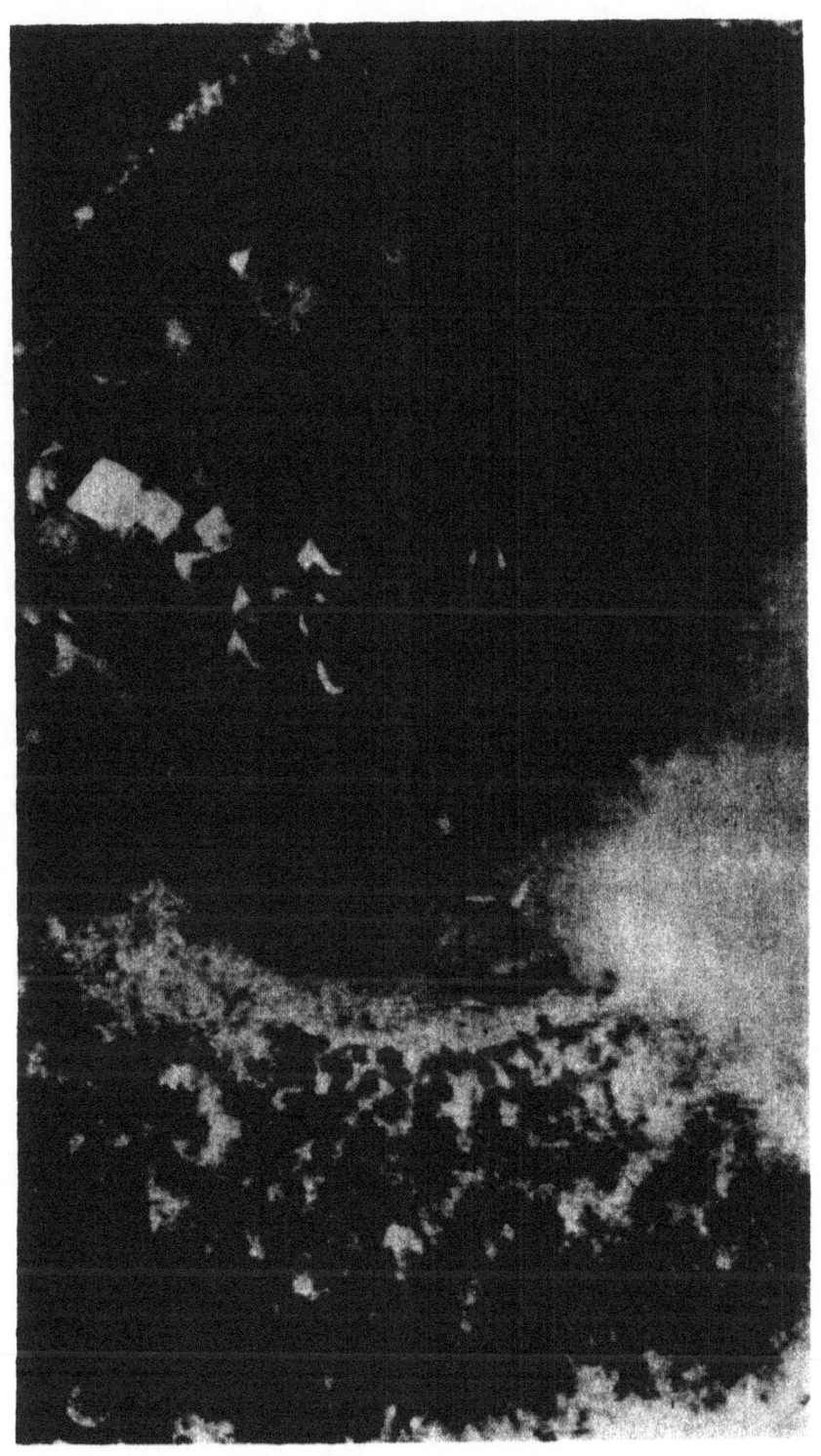

57mm NVN AAA firing at RF-101, Feb 1966.

Hostilities in the South were reaching a point that called for further action against the North. On 13 February, the President decided to begin the sustained air war against North Vietnam: Operation Rolling Thunder.

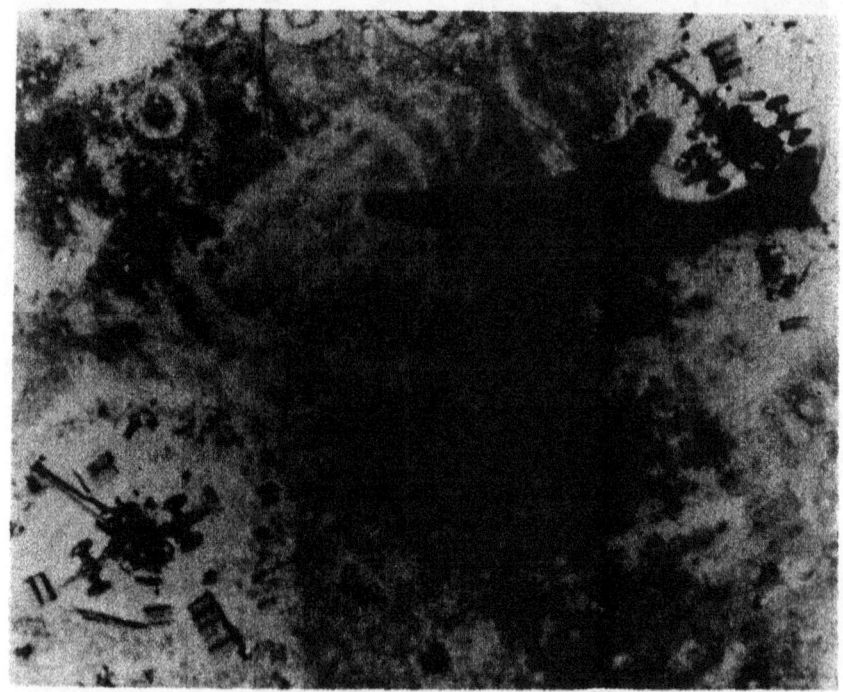

RF-101 flies over 57mm AAA weapons position in NVN, 25 Jan 1966.

Chapter III. Rolling Thunder
March 1965-December 1965

The Bombing Begins in Earnest

On 12 February 1965, the Joint Chiefs of Staff recommended an eight-week program of action against North Vietnam. They forwarded this program to the President through the Secretary of Defense. On 13, February, President Johnson authorized the operation. The code name given to this plan was Operation Rolling Thunder.

Rolling Thunder was to be a measured and limited air action, executed jointly with the government of South Vietnam, against selected military targets in North Vietnam, south of the 19th Parallel. The program called for strikes by both US and South Vietnamese aircraft against the following military targets: barrack areas, radar sites, airfields, ammunition depots, bridges, and storage areas.

The first raid was conducted on 2 March when a strike force of 44 F-105s, 40 F-100s, 7 RF-101s, and 20 B-57s, with KC-135 tankers for refueling support, struck an ammunition depot at Xom Bang. Nineteen A-1Hs of the South Vietnamese Air Force struck the Quang Khe Naval Base.

During this attack the strike forces again met what was to remain the greatest threat to air superiority throughout the entire war — antiaircraft artillery fire. The US lost four aircraft during this raid, three while attacking antiaircraft positions. Immediately, flak suppression tactics were reexamined and flak suppression was scheduled only when considered absolutely essential for protection of the primary strike force.

Another important lesson learned during this first raid was that combat losses could be reduced if pilots made only one pass on the target and then departed the area. Multiple attacks, or remaining to search for targets of opportunity invited trouble. Additionally, a smaller number of aircraft was to be used on a random recycle and restrike basis against the same target complex. This would also allow greater flexibility in tactics, more surprise, and far less exposure time per aircraft.

In mid-March, after a fact-finding mission by General Harold Johnson, the Army Chief of Staff, the President relaxed some of the bombing restrictions previously imposed. Heretofore, the President and the Secretary of Defense had day-to-day approval on all targets, even prescribing the strike dates and times. Now, although the President and Secretary continued to select targets, it was no longer on a day-by-day basis. Targets were now selected in weekly packages with the precise timing of the individual attacks left to the on-scene commander. Further changes to the ground rules permitted random armed reconnaissance of highways and railways, and flak suppression and CAP aircraft which had not expended their ordnance were permitted to attack targets enroute home from the target area.

The First MIG Attacks

On 4 April, the USAF attacked what was to prove one of the most stubborn targets of all—the Thanh Hoa railroad and highway bridge, 70 miles south of Hanoi. While striking this target, the pilots encountered a second threat to air superiority—the MIG.

The USAF employed a strike force of F-105s, supported by F-100s in a MIGCAP role, to destroy the bridge. Although the force hit the bridge with numerous bombs, not a span fell. During a restrike on the bridge the USAF lost its first aircraft to MIGs. The incident occurred as follows.

Zinc Flight, four F-105s from Korat, was scheduled to be the fourth element in the strike force. Due to refueling problems and a haze restriction to visibility, the attacking planes were not on schedule and began "bunching up" over the target. The strike, however, was under the control of a mission commander orbiting the area, and he instructed Zinc Flight to orbit over the checkpoint. Zinc Flight had been in the orbit area 10 miles south of the target, for three or four minutes and had almost completed an orbit, when the number three pilot spotted two aircraft making a diving high speed pass toward the flight. When the aircraft closed to about 3000-4000 feet, he identified them as MIGs, attacking Zinc Lead and Zinc Two. He radioed, "Zinc Lead, break—you have MIGs behind you. Zinc Lead, break. Zinc Lead, we're being attacked." Zinc Four also saw the attacking MIGs and gave a similar warning.

Neither Zinc Lead or Two reacted to the warnings, and the MIGs continued their attack. At this time Zinc Three spotted two more MIGs behind the first two. They were set up to attack Zinc Three and Four. Zinc Three called for the formation to break, and along with Zinc Four broke left into the attacking MIGs.

Meanwhile, the leading MIGs passed in front and above Zinc Three and Four. They were light grey MIG-17s with Chinese Communist red-star-and-bar markings on the bottom of the wings. The

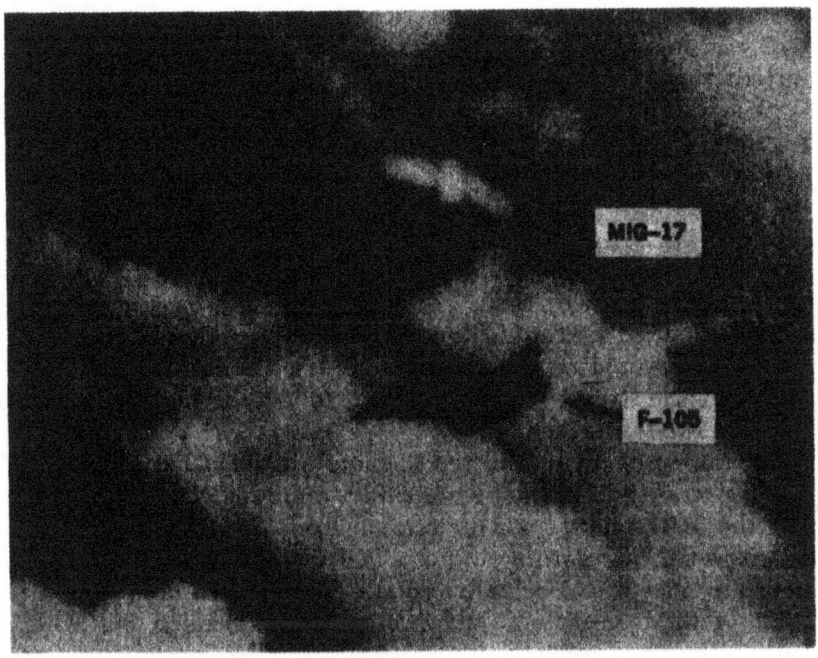
MIG-17 and F-105 in dogfight over NVN, 28 Aug 1967.

MIG leader fired his guns when he was about 1500 feet behind Zinc Lead. Zinc Three observed pieces of metal coming from the aft section of Zinc Lead's aircraft. The second MIG flying in almost a fighting wing position (200 feet out, 200-300 feet behind) fired on Zinc Two almost simultaneously. Zinc Three observed flames on the aft section of Zinc Two's aircraft. The two MIGs ceased fire at an estimated range of 700-800 feet, rolled wings level and continued straight ahead at high speed. The remaining MIGs did not attack Zinc Three and Four, but followed the first two. A MIGCAP of F-100s was unable to respond to the MIGs because the MIGCAP was protecting aircraft bombing the bridge, and haze prevented adequate visual warning of the sudden attack.

These first two losses revealed some interesting MIG tactics. Because of restricted visibility the MIG pilots were obviously using vectors from ground controlled intercept (GCI) radar to establish their six o'clock positioning. Their second tactic was the hit and run technique that was employed successfully throughout the war.

The First MIG Kills

During the second week of July 1965, the USAF achieved its first MIG kills. Although MIG activity had been light compared to what was to come, strike pilots began to detect an enemy pattern in the MIG warnings which were broadcast by the EC-121D, Big Eye, support aircraft. These aircraft, flying at low altitudes over the Gulf of Tonkin and equipped with search radar and radio relay transmitters, determined the range and altitude of hostile aircraft and issued warning to friendly aircraft.

The MIG warning at this time was given via a color code. Yellow signified that MIGs were airborne, and Red meant that MIGs were about ten minutes from a possible engagement. As a rule, the warnings would be cyclical; first, yellow, then red, and back to yellow as the MIGs feinted a return to home base. However, shortly thereafter, the warning would return to red as the last US flight departed the area after the strike. The MIGs would follow the flight out of the area, but rarely attacked.

The timing of the second red warning was such that the friendly escort aircraft had only minimum fuel remining. It was suspected that the MIG pilots could determine from their radar when the escorts would be returning to base, and when, because of their low fuel state, they would be able to make only one fast intercept. As a result of these suspicions, strike pilots recommended that USAF fighters plan tactics based on the fact that the MIGs retreated when the attack force came into the area and, if they would do combat at all, they would attack only the last flights when the escorts would be low on fuel.

As a result of this recommendation, on 10 July 1965 an escort flight of four F-4Cs from the 45th Tactical Fighter Squadron

Side view of an EC-121D aircraft of the Air Defense Command in flight near McClellan AFB, CA, 1967.

delayed their usual takeoff time until 20 minutes before the strike force departure. The escort flight then followed the last F-105 strike flight and arrived approximately 15 minutes after the other F-4 escort flights. This tactic was designed to give the 45th TFS F-4 escort flight the appearance of being the last F-105 flight over target. The flight maintained radio silence and flew the altitude and speed of the F-105 flights. The flight was spread in a formation with lead and number two on the left and three and four on the right. Flight members maintained approximately 2000 feet between the two aircraft in each element and 5000 feet between the elements. This formation was selected because it provided more coverage to the rear of the flight. The second two aircraft (second element) provided cover by weaving behind the lead element. Lead and number three used their radars extensively, while two and four had responsibility for visual search.

After establishing an orbit near the target area, the F-4s waited. When almost at BINGO fuel (amount needed to return to base with reserve) the lead pilot decided to make one more pass to the north from which the threat was expected. After completing the turn at the southern end of the orbit, he picked up a radar contact 33 miles away; shortly thereafter, his number three also got contact. The element composed of lead and number two decided to make the visual identification of the MIGs by accelerating ahead of three and four. This tactic was designed to place them seven to ten miles ahead of the second element of F-4s. This would enable the leading F-4s to break away after visual identification and permit the second trailing F-4s to fire their Sparrow missiles if the contacts proved to be hostile.

To conserve fuel, the lead element chose not to use afterburners, and the trailing element flew an "S" pattern behind the leaders. As a result of these maneuvers, when the MIGs were sighted the elements were separated by only two to three miles instead of the desired seven to ten miles. Because they were too close together, the second element could not fire a radar guided missile.

As they passed, each turned and the MIG-17s ended up attacking the second element. Both pilots in the second element lit their afterburners. Meanwhile, the MIG pilots dropped their tanks and turned very tightly behind three and four, firing as they maneuvered for position. Both F-4 crews could see the nose of the MIG light up from the muzzle flashes. Although the MIGs initially out-turned the F-4s, the F-4s were able to accelerate during the turn and gain additional separation.

Captains Tom Roberts and Ron Anderson, pilots of number four, initially flew a fighting wing position on number three, crewed by Captains Ken Holcombe and Art Clarke, but because Roberts felt that Holcombe did not have sufficient lookout protection, he broke right during the turn in an attempt to help. The MIGs split and slid by in an overshoot. Once the overshoot occurred, Captain Holcombe decided to gain separation by executing a roll to the right and putting the aircraft into a 30 degree dive. The MIG pilot tried to follow, ending up behind and three-fourths of a mile away. Holcombe accelerated, gained more separation, and turned left into the MIG, attacking it almost head-on. Due to an inoperable radar, he was unable to launch a Sparrow missile and the Mig passed head-on, firing as it went by. After the MIG passed, Ken made a slight turn to keep the enemy in sight, and then made a sixty degree dive to 10,000 feet. Since he was still in afterburner, he was able to reach 1.3 mach. He then initiated a high-G barrel roll, with the MIG having turned behind him at approximately one mile. As he completed three-fourths of the roll, he noticed the MIG firing again from the seven o'clock position. As he completed the high-G roll the MIG again overshot. This time the MIG again started to turn, but then leveled and descended towards a cloud.

Ken and Art were now about 13,000 feet at mach 0.95 with the MIG almost straight ahead. Ken fired a Sidewinder heat-seeking missile at about 1 to 1¼ mile range. He did not see the missile. He then fired a second missile, which detonated just aft of the MIG-17, destroying it. Short of fuel, he headed for recovery at Udorn.

In the meantime, Tom and Ron in the number four aircraft after breaking right, started an afterburner assisted dive from 20,000 feet. Tom accelerated to about mach 1.4 at 12,000 feet and started a 4G pull-up. During this maneuver the following MIG lost some distance but continued to follow. In the pull-up, Tom lost sight of the MIG, so he continued his climb to 33,000 feet and came back over the top, inverted in a "sort of Immelmann" to rejoin the flight. On rolling out at the top, he observed the MIG at about 28,000 feet in a 90 degree bank, doing a vertical recovery. He completed his maneuver and had the MIG about 4,000 to 5,000 feet in front of him. He fired a Sidewinder. The missile went by the MIG's tailpipe and detonated near the left wing tip. Captain Roberts fired a second missile but this one failed to track. Finally, his third Sidewinder destroyed the MIG.

Credited for the first USAF MIG kills in the air war over North Vietnam were Captain Kenneth E. Holcombe (AC), Captain Arthur C. Clarke (P), Captain Thomas S. Roberts (AC), and Captain Ronald C. Anderson (P). Total elapsed time for both engagements was less than four minutes.

SAMs and More MIGs

The USAF did not have long to enjoy its success in the air-to-air encounter. Shortly thereafter an EB-66 (a twin engine electronic counter-measures aircraft) intercepted radar signals used to guide

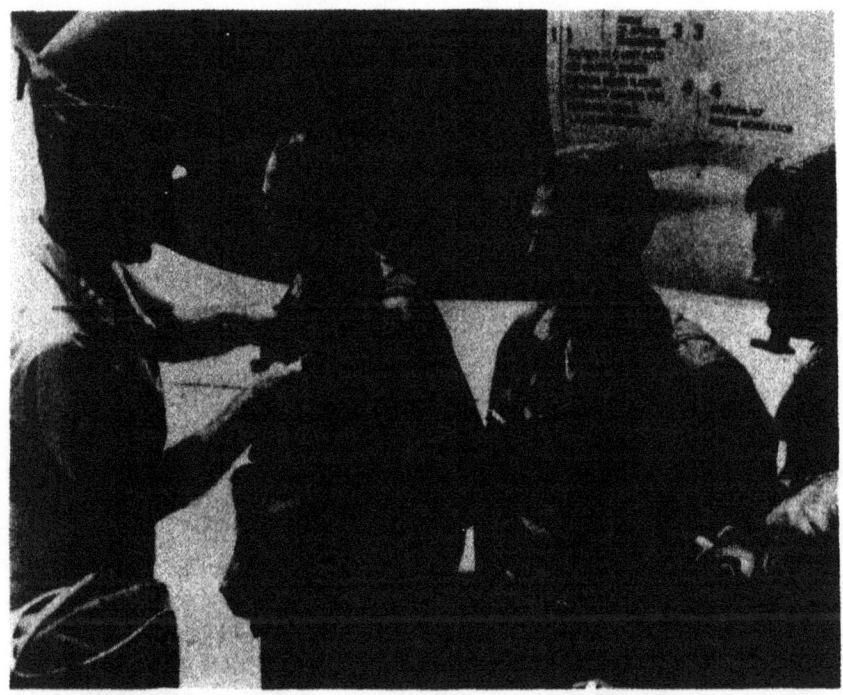

MIG Killers—Lt Gen Joseph H. Moore, Commander of the 2nd Air Division, awards Silver Star medals to F-4C aircraft commanders who downed two Communist MIG type jets over North Vietnam, on 12 Jul 1965. Accepting the awards are USAF pilots Capt Kenneth D. Holcombe of Detroit, MI, and Capt Thomas S. Roberts of LaGrange, GA.

surface-to-air missiles (SAM). This meant that the North Vietnamese were ready to use the third threat to US air superiority—the SAM. This SAM site was plotted west of Hanoi where none had been identified before. Five other suspected sites had previously been visually identified but their operational status was unknown.

Pilots preparing for strikes against NVN were briefed on the new threat. On 24 July, flights of F-4Cs from Ubon were flying MIGCAP when an EB-66 intercepted more SAM radar signals and flashed a warning to all friendly aircraft. This site was also estimated to be west of Hanoi. Shortly after the warning had been given, an F-4C pilot observed a missile climbing at an estimated speed of Mach 1, with a climb angle of greater than 50 degrees. Within seconds, he saw it hit one of the other F-4s. The aircraft disintegrated in a brown colored fireball. Two other missiles detonated behind the flight.

The remaining F-4s took evasive action and successfully recovered, but all had suffered damage from the original burst. From this encounter, it was learned that immediate, violent, evasive action was a useful tactic against the SAM. It was also learned that tight formations should be avoided in areas where SAMs were a threat.

Side view of EB-66 Destroyer on a mission over Southeast Asia.

As a result of this new threat, a new mission emerged, known as Iron Hand. The primary job of Iron Hand aircraft was to seek out and destroy missile sites. The first fighter aircraft to be modified with special missile radar detection equipment was the F-100F, called Wild Weasel I. This Wild Weasel aircraft would pick up the radar frequencies associated with the SAM sites, home onto the signal, and attack the missile launchers. The Iron Hand mission required specialized aircraft, ordnance loads, and tactics.

In August more suspected SAM sites surfaced on the target list. Efforts to locate and destroy these sites constituted a major portion of the air operation during August and September, but all known sites were unoccupied. MIG activity during these months was slow, with only a few sightings reported.

During November there was an increase in MIG and SAM activity. US aircrews sighted MIGs on ten different occasions. On 5 November, the USAF lost an F-105 to a SAM and on 7 November two flights of F-4s destroyed two occupied SAM sites. Fifteen days later two flights of Iron Hand F-105s, using terrain masking in order to reach the target undetected, destroyed two more sites. The F-105 was the second aircraft to be converted to the Iron Hand role.

Results of Rolling Thunder for 1965 showed that USAF pilots had logged about 10,570 tactical strike sorties over North Vietnam, dropping more than 80,000 tons of bombs. While conducting these sorties the USAF destroyed hundreds of vehicles, buildings, bridges, and ferries. Included in the results of the air superiority mission were the destruction of numerous AAA sites, SAM launchers, and radar sites. Factors effective in countering the MIGs included those found important in air-to-air combat in the First World War: formation integrity, good eyesight, aggressiveness, and training. Different types of formations were flown depending on the type of visual and radar coverage desired. Radar played a significant part since USAF aircraft were over enemy territory where enemy radar could vector NVN fighters onto them; therefore, the EC-121 was used to identify NVN fighters when they were airborne, and warn US aircraft of the enemy threat.

Tactics employed against the SAM included violent maneuvers, in both azimuth and elevation in order to evade the tracking missile. The USAF also began using specialized Wild Weasel aircraft and Iron Hand flights to attack missile emplacements.

The overall tactics employed against enemy air defenses were necessarily dynamic in nature. Whenever existing tactics resulted in relatively high attrition, changes were promptly made. These shifts in tactics brought changes in penetration altitudes, evasive maneuvers, delivery techniques, weaponeering, and equipment.

Chapter IV. Air Superiority Comes of Age

Status of Rival Capabilities

As seen in the preceding pages the initial phases of Rolling Thunder operations saw the buildup of US forces and the development of tactics to cope with the threat to US air superiority. During a one-month ceasefire in December 1965, many things occurred that required drastic changes in the US approach to air superiority. The cessation in the US air campaign over North Vietnam (24 December 1965 through 31 January 1966) while intended to show US willingness to negotiate, gave North Vietnam an unmolested opportunity to increase and perfect its defenses. When aerial operations resumed on 1 February 1966, US aircraft found a fully integrated AAA, MIG, and SAM defense system tied together by an effective command control network.

The numbers of SAM sites and MIGs had increased significantly over those previously encountered. Supersonic MIG-21s, with significantly better capabilities than a the MIG-15s and 17s, joined the NVN fighter force. Additionally, the AAA order of battle had mushroomed and spread into new areas.

After 1965, the USAF relied primarily on the following aircraft for Rolling Thunder operations. The F-105D was the primary strike, air-to-ground delivery vehicle; the F-105F (Wild Weasel) proved effective against the SAM installations. The F-4C was the MIGCAP, or air-to-air cover for the strike force; the D and E versions were follow-ons to the F-4C and embodied improved weapons delivery systems. The KC-135A provided in-flight refueling for the fighters; and the EB-66, EC-121, and C-130 aircraft provided the needed electronic surveillance and countermeasures support for the strike forces. In addition to the normal air-to-ground ordnance such as iron bombs and cluster bombs, USAF aircraft were equipped with Falcon, Sparrow, and Sidewinder air-to-air missiles. The F-105 and F-4E aircraft each had an internal 20mm cannon and the F-4D used the externally-mounted 20mm cannon pod. The combination of missiles and cannon gave the pilot both long and short range weapons for use in air-to-air engagements.

Rolling Thunder Resumes

The resumed bombing program was intended to stop infiltration and provide a basis for negotiations. To pursue the bombing task, the USAF had to maintain air superiority in areas where the air-to-ground mission would occur. However, the specific rules of engagement did not permit strict application of sound military doctrine. Lucrative targets were excluded due to bombing restrictions around Haiphong, Hanoi, and along the Communist Chinese border. The tasks, combined with the limiting rules of engagement, presented the Air Force with a formidable challenge: destroy, stop, or slow the supplies going south, but do so without attacking all elements of the enemy air defense system.

During the first half of 1966, US forces only engaged MIGs on the average of once a month. The SAM threat became more definite, but it was not as bad as it could have been due to the following three factors: poor missile quality, inadequately trained missile crews, and the evasive tactics and effective electronic countermeasures (ECM) used by the USAF aircrews. Regularly, the USAF aircrews avoided oncoming SAMs by jettisoning ordnance immediately and using a high "G" turning maneuver to make the missile overshoot. These evasive tactics decreased the SAM probability of kill but caused the US aircraft to abort target attacks.

To avoid SAMs, aircrews entered the target areas at low altitudes where the missiles were less effective and used the natural terrain features of North Vietnam to mask the ingressing force as long as possible. The final leg of the in-bound route would terminate with a pop-up maneuver designed to gain maximum altitude, enable the pilot to see the target, and make a dive bomb pass on it. Shortcomings to this approach were readily apparent. The low altitude route put the fighters within range of small arms and automatic weapons. The altitude gained during the pop-up maneuver put the fighter back in the lethal SAM envelope and allowed the pilot only a short time to acquire the target and release his weapons. Colonel M. S. "Sabre" Sams, 388th Tactical Fighter Wing Commander, said that ". . . numerous targets have not been hit because the strike force could not go into the target at the desired altitude and [aircrews] were forced to use 'pop-up' tactics which allow only a few seconds to acquire the target and [this] decreases bombing accuracy."

Even though the aircraft loss rate to SAMs was not high, the avoidance tactics combined with the enemy threat, reduced US target strike effectiveness. Therefore, new tactics or improved technology was needed to decrease the SAM threat to strike aircraft.

The specially equipped two-seat F-105F Wild Weasel and the Shrike missile provided the answer. The F-105F, replacing the F-100F, was a faster, longer aircraft. When the F-105F crew

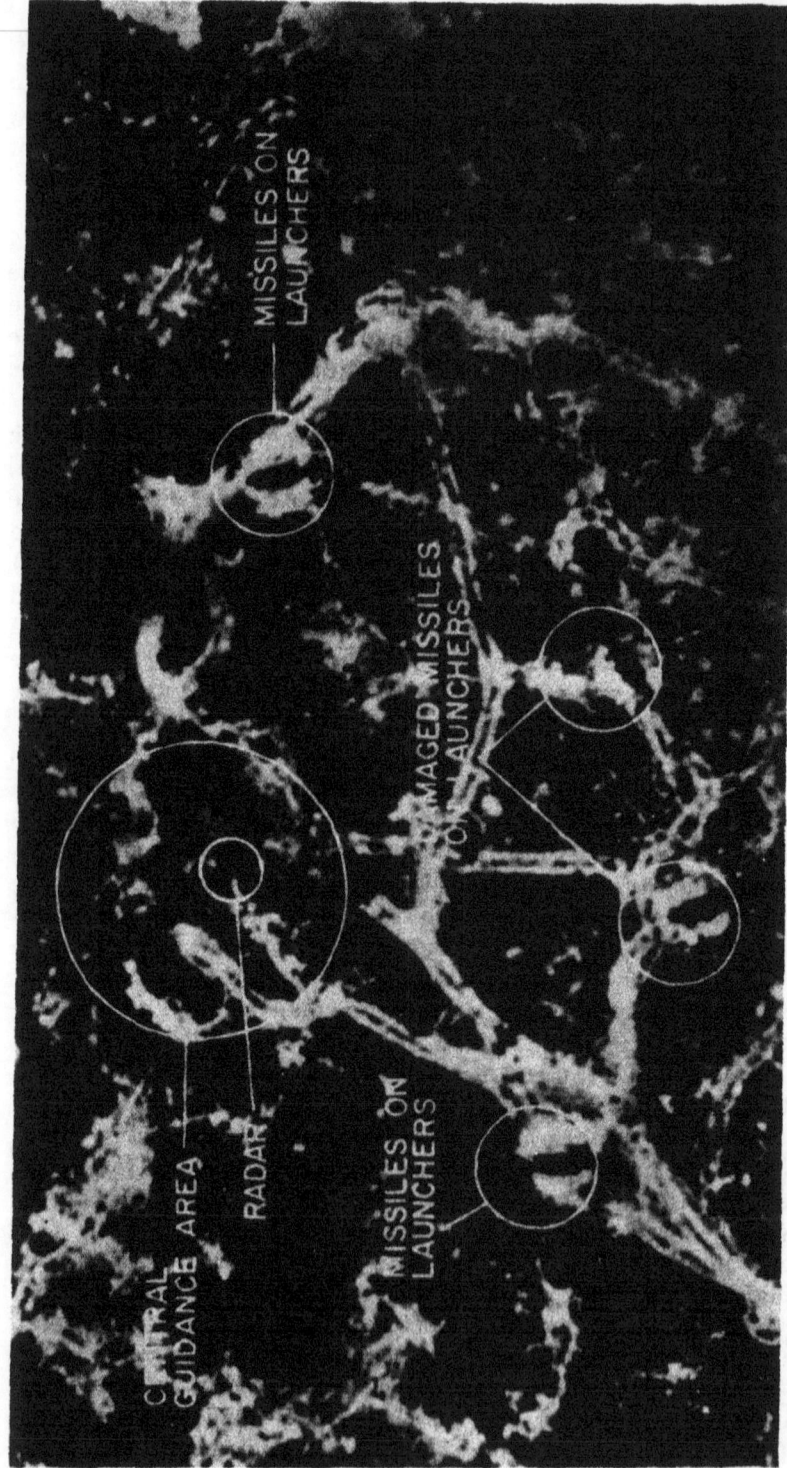

Typical SAM configuration. Destroyed by US fighter-bombers in April 1972.

detected SAM guidnace radar emissions, it would launch a Shrike beam-riding missile which guided to the radar and destroyed it. The Shrike was first used in the lesser defended portions of NVN where optimum tactics were developed. Later it was used in the heavily defended areas of the North.

With the introduction of the Shrike, the SAMs were much less effective because the time the radar operators could safely transmit was reduced considerably. For instance, to assure a high degree of accuracy, the SAM operator had to go through a comparatively lengthy sequence. First, he had to acquire the aircraft on radar, and then he had to track the aircraft from SAM launch until impact. But, if the target acquisition phase was shortened by the Shrike threat, then the SAM simply would launch at the target aircraft. In addition, if the tracking phase were also shortened, then the SAM would be fired in a far less accurate ballistic mode. For these reasons, the introduction of the Shirke had a very positive impact on reducing the SAM capability.

On 3 July 1966, a four-ship Iron Hand (SAM suppression) flight attacked three SA-2 sites in heavily defended NVN, using Shrike missiles, 2.75 inch rockets, and 20mm cannon. They attacked the first site with two shrikes, and the radar signal ceased 52 seconds after launch; destruction of this site could not be verified, however. An F-105D launched another Shrike at the second site that remained operational and probably was not hit.

The F-105F Weasel pilot then attacked the third site with a Shrike, apparently missed, and the flight had to descend to a lower altitude to avoid two SAMs that were launched at them. One missile guided on the flight but missed the aircraft by 2000 feet. The second missile closed on the Weasel, and the pilot dove to 200 feet with the missile closing. When the missile closed to an unmaneuverable point, the Weasel pilot pulled up, and the missile detonated 500 feet below him. The pilot then rolled his F-105F in on the site and strafed it, causing a secondary explosion. His wingman observed that the radar stayed on the air, so he fired a full pod of eighteen 2.75 inch rockets, that hit the radar van. Emissions ceased. Two days later on 5 July, another Iron Hand flight attacked four SAM sites. Evaluation revealed that two sites were damaged, one heavily damaged, and the fourth was destroyed.

The Wild Weasel aircraft offered the best solution at the time against the SAMs. However, the North Vietnamese soon learned how to counter the Shrike threat. SAM radars coordinated with long range EW/GCI radars to keep themselves informed of US aircraft positions. This meant that the SAM radars did not have to perform the tracking function. They stayed in a warm-up condition, called "dummy load." From these, the SAM operators switched to an active radiating position, launched the missile, and then returned to dummy load—all in a short period of time.

By such tactics, the enemy negated some of the SAM protection that the Shrike previously provided. New technology was needed to regain the upper hand. The answer was sought in electronics and the possibilities it offered. The result of the effort was the electronic countermeasures (ECM) pod. The pod had the ability to jam the enemy radar in such a way that the enemy could not determine exact aircraft range and bearing information.

Colonel William S. Chairsell, 388th Tactical Fighter Wing Commander (August 1966 to August 1967), credited the introduction of the ECM pod as the major factor allowing improved tactics, better bombing accuracy, and a reduction in aircraft loss rate. The pod allowed "Thuds" to roll in on targets from medium altitudes—12,000 to 15,000 feet—giving more positive target identification and improved weapons delivery accuracy.

Prior to the pod's integration into the F-105 weapon system, the 388th Wing conducted an operational test of its capability. During 1-8 October 1966, F-105 pilots flew numerous sorties in pod-equipped aircraft to ascertain the feasibility of new tactics for use against gunlaying and SAM radars. More than 100 successful sorties were flown with very promising results. The fighters were able to go relatively unmolested into the target area at altitudes between 10,000 and 17,000 feet. Many aircraft actually flew multiple orbit patterns in the target area, yet received no hostile fire.

On 7 October, two pod-equipped flights were bombing their assigned targets when they detected 10 AAA guidance radar signals and 12 SAM radar signals, with at least two SAM radars in the immediate target area. One flight orbited the heavy signal area at 13,000 feet prior to dropping ordnance. No missiles were fired at this flight. Far below 37mm flak was seen, but it did not appear to be directed at them.

The next day, four more F-105 flights tested the pod, but, in one flight, two aircraft did not have pods. They received 37mm, 57mm, and 85mm fire; and one SAM passed nearby. The other two F-105s in the flight had ECM pods. Crews sighted sporadic barrage flak, but no missiles. In contrast, another pod-equipped flight flew into the target area, maintained altitudes between 13,000 and 17,000 feet, and drew no flak or missiles.

The evolution of SAM evasion tactics had indeed come a long way. Heretofore, low altitude ingress to avoid SAMs created unacceptable losses from AAA and small arms. The follow-on tactic had been a change in altitude, from "on the deck" to 4,500-6,000 feet, and also meant protecting the strike force with Wild Weasels. This modification had taken the attacking aircraft out of the AAA/small arms envelope but placed them within effective SAM range. Now, with the introduction of the ECM pod, US fighters again were able to operate with some freedom within the North Vietnamese SAM environment. Colonel Chairsell went on to say, ". . . seldom has a technological advance of this nature so degraded the enemy's defense posture. It has literally transformed the hostile air defense environment we once faced, to one in which we can now operate with a latitude of permissibility." For the moment, effective tactics against the radars of SAMs and AAA guns had been perfected. However, the MIGs still remained a problem.

MIGs and Operation Bolo

In April and May of 1966, the MIG force had actively and aggressively engaged USAF forces. Their tactics indicated that support aircraft were prime targets. To combat the threat, support aircraft received F-4C MIGCAP protection.

The MIG threat would have been nullified somewhat if enemy airfields could have been attacked. However, such permission never came as a typical execution order indicated: "Not, repeat, not authorized to attack North Vietnamese air bases from which attacking aircraft may be operating." Since the MIGs could not be attacked on the ground, the USAF was forced to engage them in the air, usually on the MIG's terms.

An answer to the MIG problem came in Operation Bolo. Restricted from attacking the enemy aircraft on the ground, Air Force planners designed an operation to lure MIGs into an air battle on US terms. Colonel Robin Olds, Commander of the 8th Tactical Fighter Wing, led his unit in the execution of Operation Bolo. A major problem that had to be coped with was the unpredictable reaction of North Vietnamese air defense forces. In the past, MIG reactions to USAF airstrikes had been cyclic, perhaps geared to either the experience level of the available MIG pilots or influenced by seasonal weather and the offensive strike pattern. Aware of this predictability problem, the overall objective of Operation Bolo was formulated: destroy the airborne force of the North Vietnamese. The specific objective: deceive and lure the MIG air defense force into a reaction posture and, once airborne, seek them out, engage, pursue, and destroy them.

The attacking F-4 force would have to appear on enemy radar as a normal F-105 strike force. A typical pre-Bolo strike force consisted of F-105s in the strike role, four flights of four F-4s each for MIGCAP and also a backup air-to-ground role, plus one or two Iron Hand flights comprised of two F-105Ds and two F-105F Wild Weasels. The normal overland route went north over Laos, then over the mountains to the Red River Valley and into the target area. The

USAF RF-4C flying over Southeast Asia, 3 Aug 1971.

Col Robin Olds (far left) and pilots of the 333rd Tactical Fighter Squadron (Wolf Pack) leaving for a mission over North Vietnam. 1967.

water route went north over the Gulf of Tonkin, turned west and proceeded along the ridge line 20 miles north of Haiphong.

In Operation Bolo, F-4Cs equipped for air-to-air combat would replace the F-105s. F-4Es with an internally mounted gun were not yet available. The F-105s had been using the ECM pod, so the F-4Cs had to be similarly equipped.

The Christmas bombing halt in December 1966 provided the normal North Vietnamese buildup during the truce. On 2 January 1967, Operation Bolo, commanded by Colonel Olds, was launched. Here is Olds' description of that eventful day:

> . . . I was serving as mission commander of a force of F-4C, F-104, and F-105 aircraft performing a planned fighter sweep in the Hanoi area. Fourteen flights of F-4s, six flights of F-105 Iron Hand, and four flights of F-104s participated in the sweep, supported in the normal fashion by B-66 ECM, RC-121 Big Eye, and K-135 tankers. The B-66s were provided escort by additional F-4C aircraft.
>
> As mission commander, I flew lead position in Olds flight, first in the stream of F-4Cs planned to converge on Phuc Yen airfield. TOT (time on target) was 1400G (Greenwich), and was made good. No definite radar contacts were made as we ingressed on a heading of 145 degrees. Weather at the time was solid undercast, tops estimated 7000 feet, ceiling unknown. I led Olds' flight past Phuc Yen for approximately 14 to 18 nm (nautical miles), then turned so as to cross Phuc Yen again on a reciprocal heading. As the turn was completed Olds 3 picked up a radar contact low at 12 o'clock, high closure rate. He gained a lock-on and instructed to attack. Steering dot information put the flight into a 10 to 15 degree dive. Just as we neared the top of the undercast, radar broke lock. The target was under or in the overcast and had passed beneath us on an opposite heading.
>
> I led the flight on past the airfield once again, called the ingressing F-4 flights Ford and Rambler that missiles free was no longer in effect and turned my flight back southeast. Just as we again crossed Phuc Yen, Ford flight arrived on time. Everything then happened at once. Ford called a MIG-21 closing on Olds flight at their 7 o'clock. Olds 2 saw the MIG simultaneously. Additional MIGs were popping up through the clouds. Olds lead initiated a left turn of sufficient intensity to throw off the attacking MIG's aim, but without breaking Olds flight integrity. A defensive split by elements was automatically taken.
>
> After 90 degrees of turn in this modified break, I sighted an aircraft at my 11 o'clock in a left turn, slightly low, about a mile and a quarter away. I closed on this target for positive identification, not having seen a MIG before and by now uncertain of the exact location of all members of Ford flight. The target was positively identified as a MIG-21, silver in color, too distant for markings to be seen. I instructed the pilot (back-seater) to go bore sight, put the pipper on the target, and called for lock-

on and full system operation. I was setting us up for an AIM-7 attack. Closure was enough to necessitate haste in establishing the proper attack parameter. We achieved the steering dot (interlocks "in") and pressed-released, pressed and held the trigger. Two AIM-7s launched and appeared to track. At that moment we lost radar lock-on, having passed beyond minimum range, and the missiles had no chance to guide. I quickly selected HEAT, put the pipper on the MIG as he was disappearing into the overcast, received an indistinct missile growl and fired one AIM-9, knowing the missile had little chance to guide.

During the first encounter, Olds 2 was busily engaged in pursuing the original MIG-21 that had closed behind my flight. In addition, as I closed on the MIG that evaded in the cloud deck, I had another in sight at my 10 o'clock, in a left turn, and just above the clouds. I then turned my attention to the second MIG. I pulled sharp left, turned inside him, pulled my nose up about 30 above the horizon, rechecked my missile switches and ready panel, switched fuel to internal wing transfer, barrel rolled to the right, held my position upside down above and behind the MIG until the proper angular deflection and range parameters were satisfied, completed the rolling maneuver, and fell in behind and below the MIG-21 at his seven o'clock position at about .95 mach. Range was 4500 feet, angle off 15. The MIG-21 obligingly pulled up well above the horizon and exactly down sun. I put the pipper on his tailpipe, received a prefect growl, squeezed the trigger once, hesitated, then once again. The first Sidewinder leapt in front and within a split second, turned left in a definite and beautiful collision course correction. I did not take my eyes off the first Sidewinder and consequently did not see precisely what the second missile did. It appeared to my peripheral vision to have guided also. The first missile went slightly down, then arced gracefully up, heading for impact. Suddenly the MIG-21 erupted in a brilliant flash or orange flame. A complete wing separated and flew back in the airstream, together with a mass of smaller debris. The MIG swapped ends immediately, and tumbled forward for a few instants. It then fell, twisting, corkscrewing, tumbling, lazily toward the top of the clouds. No pilot ejection occurred above the overcast. The MIG continued to fall and disappeared into the clouds. The plan form view of the aircraft was clearly visible during many separate instants. It was minus one wing and the other presented the wedge shape, sharply swept leading edge, straight trailing edge, characteristic of the MIG-21.

I continued my left turn, looked for other MIGs, checked my fuel gage, and gave the order to egress, knowing that Olds 4, not having obtained fuel from his centerline tank, was then at bingo.

We left the battle area as Ford flight broke off its engagement and as Rambler flight became engaged.

Col Robin Olds and Capt John B. Stone return from a MIG kill over North Vietnam, 1967.

F-4 aircrews destroyed seven MIGs during Operation Bolo. No USAF Losses occurred. The new tactic, utilizing surprise by simulating the F-105s with F-4s, was effective but could not be considered long lasting. The MIG pilots, even though wary after the 2 January raid, continued to be a threat. Eventually, the MIGs became such a threat to operations that the restriction against attacking North Vietnam airfields was lifted briefly in 1967.

Moves and Countermoves

Iron Hand flights, electronic countermeasures, and counter-MIG operations were employed in various combinations as air superiority tactics evolved during the Rolling Thunder era. Tactics continued to change, albeit on a smaller scale, to suit particular situations. The remainder of this chapter illustrates the see-saw battle for tactical advantage.

At the beginning of 1967, the AAA/AW threat in North Vietnam consisted of 5000 to 7000 weapons, ranging from the 12.7mm to 100mm guns. In addition, US intelligence had identified approximately 170 SAM sites in North Vietnam. The US reacted to this increased threat by adopting special formation procedures using the jamming capabilities of the ECM pods. Pilots flew a specific flight formation position, both laterally and vertically, to gain maximum pod radiation coverage. If flight members maintained proper distances, the ECM pods denied the ground radars range, bearing, and altitude information. This effective tactic caused the North Vietnamese to begin inaccurate barrage firing with SAMs and AAA.

In May 1967, after the MIG airfields were declared valid targets, USAF fighters destroyed 26 MIGs on the ground. Strikes were timed to catch the MIGs between sorties. Another MIG deterrent came in the form of the EC-121M Rivet Top aircraft that arrived in late August 1967. This EC-121 could detect a MIG taking off and report its position to to US aircraft in the area. Colonel Howard C. Johnson, the 388th Tactical Fighter Wing Deputy for Operations, said that, "Rivet Top has provided outstanding real time MIG information to our strike force." Once again a slight tactical edge had been gained.

In an October three-day effort against the MIG, 20 were damaged or destroyed at Phuc Yen and Cat Bi airfields. But in November, the US was faced with an renewed SAM threat. The North Vietnamese installed optical tracking devices on the Sam guidance system, severly degrading the effectiveness of the ECM pod. US ECM and antiradiation missiles were upgraded, but the Rolling Thunder operation closed with a distinct possibility that the enemy had regained the upper hand in the use of the SAMs.

From mid-December 1967 to 1 April 1968, the US made no major changes in the rules of engagement or targeting. Then in early April, bombing restrictions were imposed, limiting USAF operations to only the southern portion of North Vietnam. These lower route package areas were easier to attack than the heavily defended Hanoi and Haiphong areas. Since few SAM sites were present in the south, the Iron Hand Flights found very few radar targets, and although the Iron Hand F-105s now carried a new missile, the Standard Arm, which was a vast improvement over the Shrike, they rarely had occasion to fire it.

The MIGs that operated in this area of North Vietnam did not have the GCI and SAM support that they enjoyed further North, thus, they were relegated to hit-and-run tactics. The focus of air superiority tactics improvement shifted to the research and development of improved weapons and the training associated with these weapons when President Johnson directed the bombing halt on 31 October 1968.

Air-to-Air Losses During Rolling Thunder

NVN 116
US 55

Chapter V. Bombing of the North Resumes: Operation Linebacker I

In the spring of 1972, increased NVN activity in the DMZ caused President Nixon to issue admonitions to NVN that the US would not allow an offensive to go unanswered. He stressed the use of military force against military targets in North Vietnam. In remarks on 30 April, he said that the North Vietnamese were taking great risks if they continued their offensive in the South. He was confident that he could limit strikes to military targets. He was equally confident that if the NVN did not withdraw to the North, strikes into North Vietnam would be necessary to protect the diminishing numbers of American servicemen in Vietnam.

Throughout the early spring of 1972, USAF fighter units deployed to several bases in Southeast Asia in response to mounting tension in the DMZ. With little surprise on the first of May, ground fighting intensified around Quang Tri City in the northernmost provence of South Vietnam. General Vo Nguyen Giap's numerically superior force, supported by armor and heavy artillery, took the city from 8,000 troops of the Army of the Republic of Vietnam (ARVN) 3d Infantry.

This flagrant violation of South Vietnamese territory, and the US promise of support, set the stage for renewed combat. On 4 May, the South Vietnamese and US negotiators jointly agreed to cancel indefinitely the then ongoing Paris peace talks.

On 8 May, the President ordered the mining of North Vietnamese ports. This was to support the interdiction of land routes to NVN and the resumption of naval and air strikes. The intensive air strikes into North Vietnam were to be known as Operation Linebacker.

8 May was also the day the Major Robert A. Lodge and Captain Roger C. Locher got their second MIG kill. Major Lodge was leading Oyster flight, four F-4s whose mission was to provide MIGCAP support for a major joint Navy/Air Force strike in the Hanoi area. Oyster One and Oyster Three had new improved radar sets that allowed them to detect MIGs at extended ranges. In addition, the improved Navy radar picket ship, *Red Crown*, was operating in the

147

Members of the 49th Tactical Fighter Wing during a briefing prior to their deployment to SEA, 1972.

Gulf of Tonkin. Around nine o'clock in the morning Major Lodge led his flight into North Vietnam. With the air of *Red Crown's* MIG advisories, Major Lodge and Captain Locher were developing the air picture in their minds in anticipation of the events that would follow.

There were two flights of MIGs northwest of Hanoi. One of these flights had already engaged Galore, another MIGCAP flight of four F-4s. Galore Three, with Major Barton P. Crews in the front seat and Captain Keith W. Jones, Jr. in the back seat, would also get a kill this day.

Major Lodge turned Oyster flight north; his intent was to assist Galore. They immediately identified the battle on their radar and pressed the attack. Shortly thereafter, *Red Crown* advised Oyster flight that they were being attacked by MIGs from their right. Major Lodge brought the flight around in a hard right turn to an easterly heading. Captain Locher immediately acquired the MIGs at 12 o'clock, 40 miles away. Oyster Three also identified the radar contacts, and *Red Crown* cleared Major Lodge in Oyster One to fire.[1]

Before Oyster could close to missile range, the MIGs, apparently also under ground control, turned away. Major Lodge ended up in trail with the MIGs, but just outside missile range. They continued to close but by this time the air picture had become confused. To be sure that he did not fire on friendly aircraft, Major Lodge decided to visually identify the MIGs before firing. He closed to about a mile, visually confirmed that his target was a MIG, and shot him down.

As they returned to base, Lodge and Locher reflected on the joy of painting their second red star on the side of the Phantom that had served them well — little did they realize that the price for the next kill would be the loss of their own aircraft.

Policy and Other Changes

The purpose of Linebacker was to reduce the North Vietnamese capability to wage war against South Vietnam to the greatest extent possible. In order to do this, the objective was divided into three basic tasks: (1) destroy the war-related resources already in NVN. (2) reduce or restrict NVN assistance from external sources; and, (3) interdict lines of communication to impede the movement of men and supplies into Laos and South Vietnam. The essential political difference between the Linebacker campaign and earlier Rolling Thunder operations was the President's decision to isolate NVN from external resupply.

---

[1]Throughout the war there were so many US aircraft over North Vietnam that US pilots could not fire a missile without either visual identification or clearence from a controlling agency such as *Red Crown*.

But Linebacker was different in several other ways. First, President Nixon gave the Seventh Air Force Commander considerably more latitude and flexibility in directing the aerial operation than previously permitted. Laser-guided bombs (LGB), with their increased accuracy allowed strikes on previously restricted targets. In addition, the rules of engagement were relaxed, providing more freedom of operation.

Now, the Seventh Air Force Commander usually set his own priorities, selected the targets, and determined the strike. This allowed him to consider such important factors as military priorities, weather, enemy defenses, and operational status of the target. The theater air commander also had the authority to restrike or divert strikes based on his assessment of post-strike reconnaissance. This fundamental change in management returned a portion of the process of prosecuting the war to the professional military commander in the field. Armed with greater authority, a larger target list, and the knowledge that the President wanted results, General John W. Vogt, Jr. Seventh Air Force Commander, set about accomplishing the objective of Linebacker. All targets of the Linebacker campaign fell into categories associated with the three tasks described on page

Linebacker strikes by Air Force aircraft against these targets were planned and executed decisively and concurrently with the US Navy. Each service assumed responsibility for targets within a specified area and established a completion date for destruction. They then executed the campaign. Once begun, the operation was not one of gradual escalation similar to Rolling Thunder, but was immediate and punishing. The cumulative impact was crushing.

Strikes on war-related resources destroyed vehicle repair facilities, POL storage areas, war-making industries, port facilities, SAM sites, airfields, truck parks, military storage areas, military camps, headquarters, and assembly areas. In order to "reduce or restrict NVN assistance form external sources," all main harbors of NVN were mined and the northeast and northwest rail lines were interdicted. Loss of harbors forced Soviet and Chinese ships into the time-consuming task of off-loading into shallow draft boats or barges outside the 12-mile limit. This "lightering" process extended the unloading time for a five or six thousand ton vessel to more than a month. Thus, the mining made resupply from ships relatively insignificant. On land, the northeast and northwest rail lines were the primary land routes from China. Continuing strikes also insured that these resupply channels were reduced to a trickle.

Tactical airpower accomplished the last task, "interdicting the lines of communication to impede the movement of men and materials into Laos and South Vietnam," by systematically striking bridges, key choke points, port facilities, truck parks, staging areas, POL facilities, supply caches, and trucks moving from Hanoi south.

The effect of the Linebacker campaign on these supply routes was dramatic; the enemy's supply was reduced to an estimated 20 percent of his initial capabilities.

Technological advances in weaponry contributed a large part to the success of Linebacker. Guided bombs, with their excellent accuracy, greatly increased target destruction capabilities. This significantly reduced the number of sorties required to destroy a given target, and therefore allowed the US to attack more targets. The most effective of the guided weapons was the laser guided bomb. The LGB was a conventional bomb fitted with a guidance package which steered the bomb to impact directly on a target. The target was pinpointed by an aircraft fitted with a laser designator. So accurate was this bombing system that in two days, 10 and 12 May 1972, the Air Force and Navy dropped six bridges, including the famous Hanoi Railroad and Highway Bridge, known as the Paul Doumer Bridge. And on 13 May, F-4 laser bombers completely destroyed the Thanh Hoa Bridge, billed as "the bridge which would never go down." These bridges had withstood hundreds of sorties and thousands of bombs since 1964. A few aircraft carrying LGBs had reduced them to rubble.

In addition, the LGB provided the opportunity to strike several important bridges along the northeast and northwest railroads that previously had been restricted from bombing because of their proximity to the People's Republic of China (PRC). The earlier restriction had been imposed because of possible political repercussions should the PRC receive damage from the relatively inaccurate conventional bombs. The explicit accuracy of the LGB eliminated that risk, and thus allowed destruction of these targets.

Air Superiority Enters a New Phase

By 11 May, the tempo of the conflict obviously had increased. Since the President initiated the campaign, some 1800 sorties had been flown, and the air-to-air combat box score was seven US aircraft down vs eleven MIGs.

During the combat lull prior to Linebacker, the North Vietnamese rebuilt their defenses while the US applied technology and perfected tactics which increased its offensive capability to protect strike forces. During the six months of Linebacker I (May-October 1972), the technology and tactics were introduced to counter the defensive moves of the enemy.

With Linebacker came the mission specialization of aircrews, even within the same squadron. In the past, the fighter pilot had been a "jack-of-all-trades;" a bombing mission today, counter-air operations tomorrow, and a night attack another time. But because of the moves and counter-moves on each side and the increasing degree of sophistication involved in each area of expertise, specialization became increasingly important to mission accomplishment. For example, North Vietnamese defenses forced the US to concentrate specific fighter forces on SAM and AAA suppression. LGBs required special delivery tactics and laser designator knowledge. And most important, survival and effectiveness in the air-to-air combat role required a high degree of proficiency that could only be achieved by specialized training and experience.

Under this concept, the 432d Tactical Reconnaissance Wing at Udorn, Thailand, performed the task of providing the primary MIGCAP and escort aircraft for Operation Linebacker. Within that wing, the 555th Tactical Fighter Squadron, known as the "Triple Nickel," operated as the primary counter-air squadron. This enabled the crews to fly together over extended periods, develop flight tactics, and solidify themselves as fighting units.

Successful air-to-air combat requires that all flying skills: leadership, knowledge of enemy tactics, flight discipline and integrity, mutual support, teamwork and individual capabilities be peaked. Even though many improvements in tactics and equipment greatly aided success in Linebacker, the air-to-air combat score nevertheless indicated a deficiency in pilot air-to-air combat proficiency. For while the US still maintained the advantage in the kill ratio, it had dropped considerably from the 12 to 1 kill ratio in Korea. The Air Force immediately increased its aerial combat training. Even though the results were not available in time to affect the outcomes of Linebacker I operations, the overall impact is that there is now a continuing program to prepare pilots for future air-to-air combat.

The strike package was perhaps the significant key to the success of Operation Linebacker. It normally consisted of 32 F-4s, carrying a mix of LGBs and conventional bombs, and was supported by another 20-to-40 aircraft to protect the package from the enemy defenses. While the accuracy of the LGB allowed a considerably reduced number of bombers to destroy a given target, the vulnerability of the LGB aircraft to SAMs and MIGs during weapon delivery required an increase in the number of protective support aircraft. The objectives were to inflict as much enemy damage as possible, and then bring everybody home. A tremendous amount of effort went into achieving these objectives.

The support package of a typical Linebacker strike consisted of one or two flights of F-4s configured for air-to-air escort against the immediate MIG threat, a flight of four F-4s or F-105 Wild Weasels proceding the flight in search of SAMs, a hunter-killer team of two F-105s and two F-4s in the SAM and flak suppression role, and two flights of four F-4s in the MIGCAP role. In addition, a chaff delivery flight and its escorts preceded this complex formation. The chaff flight consisted of four-to-eight A-7s or F-4s, and was escorted by a flight of F-4s and possibly a Wild Weasel and a MIGCAP flight. "Alone, unarmed, and unafraid," a single or a pair of RF-4C reconnaissance aircraft followed the strike to record target damage.

This combination of strike and support packages made up the primary Linebacker strike force. In addition, an array of ships and aircraft remained on the periphery to further support the operation. EB-66s conducted standoff ECM jamming; the RC-121, callsign DISCO, maintained radar coverage and acted as airborne command and control, as did *Red Crown,* a US Navy control ship stationed in the Gulf of Tonkin.

KC-135, Strategic Air Command tankers, refueled the strike force in-bound to the target and were available for egress refueling if required. Also standing by in case they were needed were the A-7D "Sandys" and the CH-53 "Jolly Green Giants" rescue force. The support/strike ratio ran as high as five-to-one on missions where the US anticipated strong opposition.

Linebacker missions staging out of Thailand typically ingressed NVN near Hon Gay for the Gulf of Tonkin, or through "Gorilla's Head" on the Laotian border. Usual force composition sent against any one target numbered more than 50 aircraft.

The first aircraft into the target area were the Wild Weasel and hunter-killer teams. These specially equipped aircraft detected, located, and destroyed SAMs and associated radars likely to threaten the chaff flight or the strike force. They also provided warnings to the strike crews of SAM launches.

When the Weasels were mated with F-4s carrying cluster bombs and iron bombs, they formed the hunter-killer team. Additionally, the F-4 carried air intercept missiles, and its second role was to protect the Wild Weasel element from MIG attack.

The chaff bombers were next in, following the hunter-killer by two or three minutes. Chaff bombing was a new Linebacker tactic. Their job was to spread chaff through which the vulnerable strike force bombers could fly. The chaff masked strike aircraft from enemy radars and helped prevent SAM shoot-downs. These F-4s, or A-7s, with a full load of chaff bombs, were not maneuverable and needed 30 to 50 miles of uninterrupted airspace to do their job. To protect themselves from SAMs, all chaff aircraft used ECM equipment to jam the SAM radar. This gear was carried in pods under the aircraft and required the pilots to fly a precise "pod formation" to prevent enemy radar from pinpointing any one flight member. However, flying in "pod" was not a good defense against MIGs and thus required fighter escort to counter that threat. At least one fourship escort flight of F-4s trailed the chaffers by a couple of miles on each flank. Their job was to stay with the chaffers and protect them from MIG attack from the rear.

Escort flight crews had to resist being decoyed away by tantalizing

Three F–4Es and two F–4Ds heading for refueling, Oct 1972.

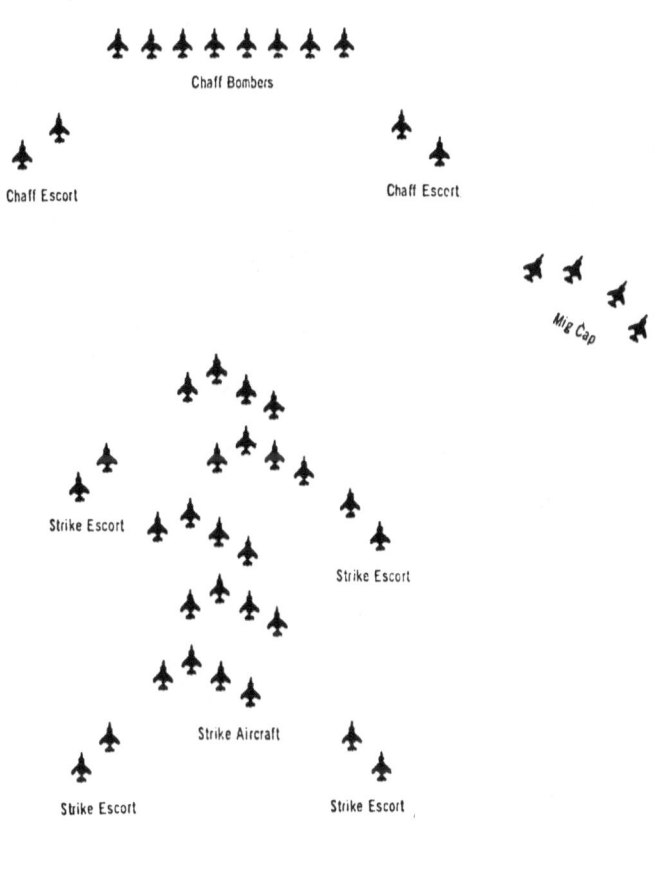

Typical linebacker strike/support package: 52 aircraft.

radar targets. They had to predict whether the MIGs seen on their radars were decoys, or whether they were a serious threat to the force. Unseen MIGs might be waiting to attack the chaff flight as soon as the escort began pursuit of the decoy. The escort flight remained with the strike force for MIG protection, while the MIGCAP was cast in an aggressive, offensive role. It attempted to search out the MIGs and engage them before they could reach the strike flight.

Patrolling the ingress track, the MIGCAP flights would try to anticipate the direction from which the MIGs would most likely attack

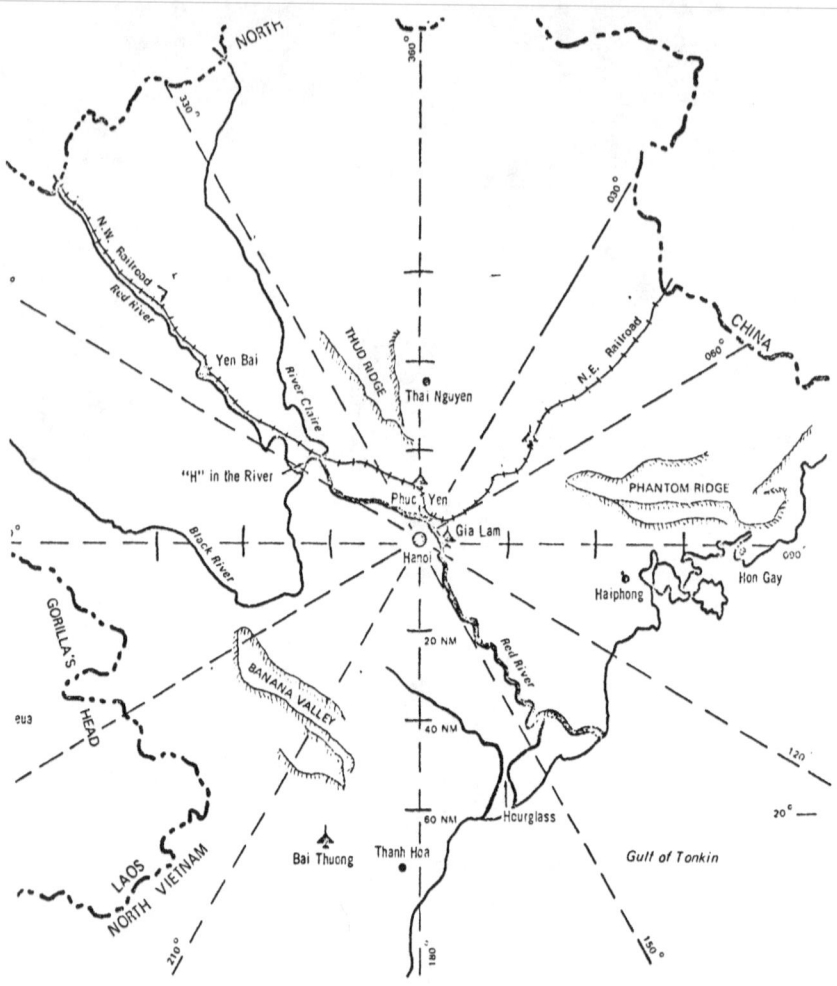

Generalized map of the air-to-air combat arena.

the force. The flight leader could then set up an orbit pattern to most effectively protect the strike flights. The strike force followed the chaff package by about 15 minutes in order to give the chaff time to disperse. The force entered the area virtually surrounded by protection: by chaff, by escorts, by Weasels, and by the roving MIGCAP.

At the beginning of Linebacker, May 1972, US intelligence estimates placed the North Vietnamese air order of battle at 250 MIGs one-third of which were the newer MIG-21. The enemy also had nearly 300 strategically placed SAM sites imbedded in the ground and better than 1500 AAA weapons defending the most important targets. This massive threat to US aircrews was tightly integrated through the use of some of the best Soviet communications and radar equipment and enjoyed the distinct advantage of operating over its own homeland. Although AAA still provided the greatest threat at low altitudes, the biggest challenge was to protect the force form SAMs and MIGs. Technology again helped accomplish the job.

Technology Versus Enemy Defenses

Electronic identification of enemy aircraft allowed MIG hunters to take full advantage of the head-on capabilities of the US radar-guided, air-to-air missile. Previously, the rules of engagement required US pilots to identify MIGs visually before firing at them. Now, new aircraft equipment allowed positive electronic identification, eliminating the likelihood of extended maneuvering with agile MIGs.

The electronic capability to stand-off and shoot was enhanced by the improved dog-flight Sparrow and Sidewinder air-to-air missiles incorporating quicker reaction, greater range, and more maneuverability. Another technological advance was the adaptation of the F-4E, Phantom II, with a SAM hunting capability comparable to the F-105 Wild Weasel. The F-4 was more maneuverable, and if engaged by MIGs, had a better chance of success.

Defensive technological advances against the SAM included improved ECM pods and the use of chaff. The new ECM pods provided jamming over a wider selection of frequencies than previously possible. This, the electronic "music" that these pods emitted, was able to counter a variety of radar and electronic signals. Chaff was also very effective when used to counter GCI and SAM radars. However, in 1972, it was really a reapplication of technology, having been used for similar purposes in World War II.

As previously discussed, chaff was employed to protect the strike force. Increasingly, however, pilots used it to protect their individual aircraft. They tucked chaff bundles into the speed brake compartments of their fighters. When a SAM was fired at the flight, a pilot would open his speed brakes and deploy his chaff bundles into the slip stream, causing the missile to guide on the chaff rather than on the missile-dodging aircraft.

Technology also affected the evolution of tactics against the MIGs. Control and warning capabilities were advanced by integrating an airborne radar aircraft and the US Navy's radar ship, with a computer site in Thailand. These systems formed an effective network of MIG watch warnings to counter the enemy fighter threat.

Every perceived threat was weighed for possible counter-measures. These and all other efforts of the Air Force, Navy, and Marine Corps

F-4s being refueled by SAC KC-135, Oct 1972.

tactical air effort were fully coordinated among Admiral John S. McCain, Jr., Commander-in-Chief, Pacific Command; General Frederick C. Weyand, US Army Commander, Military Assistance Command, Vietnam (MACV); and General John W. Vogt, Jr, USAF Deputy Commander of MACV. These communications improved aircraft employment throughout the theater.

Oyster Flight on a Linebacker Mission

On 10 May 1972, Major Robert Lodge again led Oyster flight into battle. This would be his last flight. The strike package consisted of 32 F-4s in the attack role, plus the normal support aircraft. Twelve of the strike planes were armed with the new laser guided bombs, four carried electro-optical guided bombs (EOGBs) and sixteen were loaded with conventional 500 pound bombs. The targets included the Paul Doumer Bridge and the Yen Vien Railroad Yard. Since they were near "downtown" Hanoi, pilots expected a vigorous MIG reaction.

The operation was complex and required precise timing and coordination. The strike and support aircraft came from several bases, consolidating as units during aerial refueling, and then heading north as complete packages.

Oyster refueled routinely and headed North. Major Lodge, and his backseater, Weapon Systems Officer (WSO), Captain Roger C. Locher were leading a highly experienced eight man team. They had worked together frequently and each knew his assignment. Bob Lodge and Roger Locher had been together for over eight months. Both had previous Southeast Asia combat tours, and had two recent MIG kills to their credit.

Major Lodge's wingman, Oyster Two, was 25-year old First Lieutenant John D. Markle, a veteran of 78 combat missions; twenty were over North Vietnam. His WSO was Captain Stephen D. Eaves. Captain Richard S. "Steve" Ritchie, with Captain Charles B. "Chuck" Debellevue as the WSO, flew number 3 aircraft, leading the second element.

Later Steve Ritchie would become the first USAF Ace of the Vietnam conflict with five kills, and Chuck Debellevue would become the first ever USAF navigator Ace. Debellevue became, in fact, the leading USAF Ace of the war being credited with six kills. Ritchie's wingman, Oyster 4, was Lieutenant Tommy Feezel, another young man who had rapidly gained experience and proved himself. His WSO was Captain Lawrence Pettit.

As Oyster flight approached NVN, the leader of Balter flight, the other MIGCAP flight for the mission, told Major Lodge that two of his flight members had aborted and the flight would be late arriving

Captains Steve Ritchie and "Chuck" Debellevue stand beside their F-4 with five red stars signifying their Ace status, Oct 1972.

at its patrol area. Balter flight was delaying to pick up a spare aircraft. Major Lodge, aware of the probable MIG opposition, decided to cover both patrol areas, thus providing maximum protection for the strike force.

Oyster flight, heading east-northeast, crossed into NVN at the Gorilla's Head and proceeded towards its patrol area near Hanoi 80 miles away. The object was to stay between the MIGs, just getting airborne, and the strike flight. The visibility was good and only a few puffy clouds hung over Thud Ridge and the hills to the west. The strike flight should easily find the target, but clear weather also meant the MIGs would be up in force.

En route to the patrol area, Oyster flight members jettisoned their centerline fuel tanks as they went dry, descended to 3,000 feet above ground level, and accelerated to 500 kts. High airspeed was most important in this environment and they never let it get low. They needed that airspeed to evade a SAM or a missile, or outmaneuver lighter and better-turning MIGs. Speed also reduced the probability of an AAA hit. They were going into the target area low and fast.

Red Crown, on station in the Gulf of Tonkin, provided MIGCAP radar information. Therefore, as Major Lodge and his flight left the foothills, they switched to the MIGCAP frequency and established radio contact with *Red Crown.* About 40 miles out of Hanoi, Oyster flight turned northwest and was on station. Everyone was quieter now. Oyster flight, in the heart of enemy territory at low altitude, was carrying the fight directly to the enemy. Each man had specific responsibilities, knew his duties well, and the flight functioned as a team. The formation was widely spread in order that the two wingmen, Oyster 2 and 4, could provide better visual coverage against MIGs that might try to attack from six o'clock. Cockpit switches were already set up hot, but another check made certain, and then all eyes shifted outside to check for MIGs.

Suddenly, *Red Crown* advised the flight of MIG activity in the Hanoi area. But, as yet, nothing appeared on the F-4s' radar scopes. The flight continued northwest. As Oyster flight approached 30 miles south of Yen Bai airfield, Balter flight members checked in on the radio. Balter flight was about 40 miles short of its orbit point and headed in-bound. The strike force was about 20 miles left of Balter, in-bound at 15,000 feet. Oyster flight was now well ahead of all other friendly aircraft in the area. This position, and the capability to electronically identify hostile aircraft, meant that Oyster flight could fire their radar missiles in a head-on attack without having to visually identify the MIGs. This was very important. It gave the initial advantage to the F-4s because the MIGs did not have a missile designed for a head-on attack.

Shortly after Balter's position report, Captain Locher in the backseat of Oyster One got several radar contacts, indicating intensive MIG activity. As Captain Locher recalls: "The MIGs made one turn back to the north, then when they were about 45 miles from us, they all at once started heading south [at full throttle]."

Since Oyster flight was low, around 2000 feet AGL, Major Lodge elected to snap up. The MIGs were between 13,000-16,000 feet altitude and heading southeast. Radar revealed four MIGs: pairs about a mile in trail. Captain Locher locked onto the front target. Major Lodge told the element to take·the third MIG on the scope. Oyster flight had just crossed the Red River at a point 15 miles south of Yen Bai and the setup was excellent for a front quartering shot, left to right. Major Lodge and Captain Locher decided to shoot one missile at a time because on the mission two days before, they had fired two missiles at one MIG and both had hit.

Oyster flight lit the engine afterburners and started a climb to center the "aim-dot" and obtain an optimum radar firing solution. At eight miles, with a closure rate over 1000 knots between the F-4s and the MIGs, Major Lodge fired his first missile. It started to guide toward the lead MIG, but it exploded in front of Major Lodge when it armed. He immediately fired his second missile. The range was down to about six miles and the missile began to guide. After approximately five seconds there was a huge red/orange explosion; Bob Lodge and Roger Locher had their third MIG kill.

Oyster 2, crewed by Lieutenant John Markle and Captain Stephen Eaves, in fighting wing formation position on the right side of Oyster Lead, had an early radar lock-on and confirmed the bandits. As they started the snap up and Oyster Lead's missile fired, Markle checked with Eaves to insure they still had a good radar lock-on. Everything was fine and, since they were approaching the heart of the firing envelope, John Markle ripple-fired two missiles.

The missiles roared out 15 degrees right and impacted behind the canopy of the MIG-21. The first missile cut the enemy aircraft in half. Immediately, the air filled with enemy missiles, fired unguided and head-on from the remaining MIGs. Obviously, this was a diversionary tactic by the trailing MIGs, because the heat seeking missile was not a head-on weapon.

The missiles streaked over Oyster flight, followed very closely by the third MIG-21, which, to Roger Locher, seemed to come out of nowhere and almost hit him. Instinctively, Bob Lodge pulled hard to the right and found himself at six o'clock to the third MIG, but at a range of 200 feet, he was much too close for his missiles to be effective.

If Major Lodge's F-4D had had a gun, he would have used it, but he was close, even for that. He had to get some separation to give the missile time to guide and arm. The MIG began climbing in a fairly gentle two-to-three "G" right hand turn. Major Lodge followed him, planning to stay slightly to the outside of the turn, in order to gain separation as they pulled through near the top of the maneuver.

At the time Markle and Eaves had fired at the first MIG, Captains Ritchie and Debellevue in the number three position were wide to the left, and in good position to converge on the trailing MIG element. What they saw was a sky rapidly filling with activity. In Captain Ritchie's words, "Things really got confusing once the engagement started. There were missiles in the air all over the place, fireballs, smoke trails, debris, and airplanes everywhere. Lead and 2 got their kills head-on, then we converted to the six o'clock on the two remaining MIGs." He started the conversion, using radar information, with a moderate 4-to-5 "G" climbing right turn, and completed it visually. Lieutenant Tommy Feezel was on his wing in good position, but could function only as a set of eyes because his radar had failed, making his radar guided missiles useless.

As Ritchie and Debellevue completed their conversion, they saw both MIGs. Ritchie elected to take the one on the left that was flushed about 10,000 feet from the other MIG-21 and appeared to be trying to join up. The whole flight was turning right and down now. All was as it should be, the flight was 30 seconds old, Oyster flight had claimed two kills and was still behind the MIGs, well in control of the situation.

Steve Ritchie placed his sight on the MIG in front of him, switched

First Lt John D. Markle, aircraft commander and MIG killer, 555 TFS, Sep 1972.

the fire control system to auto-aquisition, and got a good radar lock-on. He waited a few seconds to insure that the release conditions of the missile had been met and ripple-fired two radar missiles. He was in good position on the MIG, about 1000 feet below and 6000 feet behind him on the inside of his turn at 18,000 feet altitude. As Steve squeezed the trigger, the MIG began to tighten his turn. The first missile came off and guided to the target, but went under the MIG and did not detonate. The second missile hit the MIG square in the center of the fuselage causing it to explode in another spectacular fireball. The MIG pilot ejected.

Captain Ritchie looked to the right in his four o'clock position and saw Lodge and Locher about 7000 feet out immediately behind their MIG and trying to drop back into firing range. Lieutenant Markle was right with him in good formation position. Suddenly, as if out of nowhere, four MIG-19s attacked Lodge and Locher.

"Oyster Lead you have MIGs at your ten o'clock." Markle and Eaves had seen the MIGs as they overshot and then pulled hard back into Oyster Lead's six o'clock position. Oyster 2 called the MIGs at ten o'clock and again at nine o'clock. Major Lodge must have thought that he could still get the MIG-21 or had not heard the radio calls because he continued to track the MIG in front. The MIG-19s quickly stabilized at about 2000 feet on Lead and opened fire with their cannon.

Almost simultaneously, Major Lodge fired his third AIM-7. But he was still too close and the missile was ineffective. Oyster 2 made a last desperate call, "Hey Lead, break right, break right, they are firing at you." The MIG-19s were flying so close it was as if they were flying formation on Lead. They just kept shooting.

Oyster 2 saw Lead get hit and explode. Captain Locher the WSO ejected. Markle and Eaves disengaged, went full afterburner and sliced down and out of the flight. Picking up a heading of 310 degrees on the deck and checking their six o'clock for other MIGs, Oyster 2 departed the area.

Oyster 3 and 4 also turned for home. They lit their afterburners and headed for the deck, indicating 650 knots airspeed. Lieutenant Feezel spread wide on Ritchie for better mutual support and began looking for other aircraft in the area. As they crossed the ridge line just west of the Red River at about 50 feet altitude, Lieutenant Feezel saw a MIG-21 about 500 feet above him and 100 feet back. Obviously the MIG had not seen him. All Feezel needed to do was to go idle power and use his speed brakes to flush the MIG out front of him. Unfortunately, his radar was inoperative and, since the F-4D had no gun, he could not fire on the MIG.

Quickly he radioed Steve Ritchie about the MIG. Captain Ritchie looked out to his right, ". . . and there was 4 in my four o'clock, 5000 feet out with a shining silver MIG-21 just sitting right on top of him. I think GCI was vectoring him out after us and he just could not see us. Suddenly I looked forward just as one of those tremendous rain forest trees seemed to fill my windscreen; I put the stick in my lap and then in one corner and just missed it."

The MIG pilot pulled off to the left and rolled over to look down, but apparently still didn't see either 3 or 4. As he was probably getting low on fuel and rapidly farther from his base, he turned back to the right and departed. Lieutenant Feezel joined up on Ritchie as they climbed out towards the tanker, where they were joined by Lieutenant Markle. They would go the last few miles as a three ship formation.

Oyster 1 would not come home that night. Major Bob Lodge, an outstanding officer and a courageous leader, was killed in the line of duty. Captain Locher bailed out of the crippled Phantom just prior to its explosion and evaded capture in the NVN jungle for 23 days before a combat rescue team reached him.

In addition to the loss of Major Lodge and his F-4, Harlow 4, of the strike force escort flight, was lost, Another MIG-19, using hit and run tactics, shot down the second F-4. But Oyster flight destroyed three MIG-21s, and in conjunction with the other support aircraft accomplished its mission of protecting the strike force. The strike force reached the target and inflicted severe damage to the enemy. The F-4s carrying the conventional bombs, successfully iso-

Capt Roger C. Locher after rescue from the jungle north of Hanoi. 7AF Commander, General Vogt is in the background, 10 May 1972.

lated the Yen Vien Railroad Yard by cratering both entrances to the marshalling area. The aircraft carrying guided-bombs dropped four spans on the Paul Doumer Bridge, knocked out one abutment, and severed an adjacent rail line. The box score for the first Linebacker strike was three MIGs destroyed versus two F-4s lost; and the strike force had been highly successful.

USAF daytime losses during Linebacker 1 amounted to 44 aircraft — 12 to SAMs, 5 to AAA, and 27 to MIGs — dramatically pointing out the effectiveness of the NVN air defense system which forced the US to use more than half of the total force in the role of defense suppression. The Americans were able to do this on a daily basis, thereby maintaining air superiority continually over NVN.

A Hunter-Killer Mission Against Combined Air Defenses

The following paragraphs describe how F-4 and F-105 pilots coordinated their anti-SAM tactics. This mission also illustrates a bold new North Vietnamese move — coordinating SAM firings with MIGs in a concerted attack.

On 2 September 1972, Eagle flight finished refueling with the strike force and began a gentle descent to gain airspeed and get down to an advantageous fighting altitude. Eagle was one of two hunter-killer flights assigned to protect a Linebacker strike against Phuc Yen Airfield. Eagle 1 and 2, F-105Gs carrying anti-radiation missiles (ARMs), accelerated to the northwest of the ingress route. Eagle 3 and 4, F-4Es armed with cluster bombs, Sparrow air-to-air missiles, and a 20mm cannon, eased off to the southeast of track. Eagle ingressed two minutes ahead of the strike force at 15,000 feet, cruising at 425 knots, about 50 miles west of Hanoi. All flight members constantly cross-checked their formation positions, and monitored telltale gauges and audio signals for signs of SAM activity. The flight members were line-abreast with Eagle 2 and 4 on the outside of the formation about 2,000 feet from each element lead. Eagle 3 maintained about 5000 feet separation on Eagle Lead.

As the flight crossed the Black River about 45 miles from Hanoi, Eagle Lead's radar warning instruments picked up the first strong SAM activity signals from the target area. Eagle 1 and 2 turned and launched ARMs at the active SAM site; Eagle 3 spotted a SAM launch at ten o'clock low. Banking back into the SAM, Eagle flight dispensed speed brake chaff and evaded the SAM that detonated 200-300 feet behind Eagle 3. No one had received an electronic indication of that SAM launch. Major Jon I. Lucas and First Lieutenant Douglas C. Malloy, the Eagle 3 crew, counted four other SAMs, all launched without radar warning indications. Lucas and Malloy visually located the site. Eagle Lead cleared the F-4E element, Eagle 3 and 4, to attack while he and Eagle 2 moved off to hold near Thud Ridge about 25 miles north of the target. Eagle 3 and 4 rolled in on target from the south. Major Lucas was narrowly missed by a SAM while, simultaneously, 57 and 85mm AAA opened up on him and his wingman.

Unscathed, Eagle 3 and 4 pulled off the target and streaked north to rejoin Eagle Lead and 2. At this point the radio began crackling with MIG warnings to the strike force. Major Lucas recounts: "I heard the call 'White bandits attacking, Phuc Yen.' Following this, I heard (Eagle) 2 call that he just had a missile go by, and "break right!" Racing to support the F-105s, Major Lucas and his wingman had numerous radar warning and AAA indications. They constantly watched, and jinked violently to avoid flak.

Within minutes, Eagle 3 and 4 covered the air miles separating the two elements and saw Eagle 1 and 2 about six miles ahead. The geometry of their high speed turn to reform the flight brought them well inside the attack angle being set up by the much smaller, and not yet visible, MIG-19 that was chasing Eagle 1 and 2. Apparently, the MIG pilot was concentrating on repositioning on the F-105s in order to shoot his second missile, because when Eagle Three saw the MIG, he found himself slightly ahead and low in the MIG's eleven o'clock position. Eagle 3 and 4 pulled into a 6G turn toward the bandit in order to roll out at his six o'clock, as he streaked overhead apparently intent on his own attack on Eagle 1 and 2.

Major Jon Lucas scurried frantically in preparation for his missile attack on the MIG-19. Manipulating power and maneuvering the aircraft, he simultaneously carried on a conversation with his backseater to insure radar lock-on. Checking his missile status panel and master-arm switch, he verified a good radar lock and maneuvered his aircraft to stay in range. As the nose drifted down to the MIG's six o'clock position, Lucas squeezed the trigger.

At this point Eagle 4 called a SAM launch at two o'clock. Eagle 3 responded by breaking down into the SAM, forcing it to pass overhead. When he rolled back to locate the MIG-19, all he saw was a pastel-orange parachute.

Reconstructing the flight, it was apparent that as the MIG pressed his attack, Eagle One and Two tried to outrun the MIG. The pilot of Eagle Two recalled that he thought the MIG was going to maneuver to reattack Eagle Lead, but then he saw the MIG suddenly break to the left and disengage. The next thing he observed was the MIG spinning and smoking until it hit the ground. Lucas had shot him out of the sky.

As the battle developed across the countryside, with the two F-105s being chased by the MIG-19 who was himself being trailed by the F-4s, the North Vietnamese launched a SAM and barely missed the F-4s. North Vietnamese weapon system integration seemed sufficiently reliable to fire a SAM even with MIGs within range. It was almost a successfully coordinated defensive effort.

Later, the Red Baron study cited this mission as a classic example of mutual support. Coordination between flight members had negated the effect of the SA-2 and MIG attacks and contributed to the destruction of the MIG-19.

Eagle flight, and especially Major Jon I. Lucas and First Lieutenant Douglas C. Malloy, had performed magnificantly to thwart multiple threats.

Sowing Protective Corridors

As Oyster and Eagle flights demonstrated, the MIGCAP hunted the MIGs offensively and the hunter-killer aggressively attacked threatening SAM batteries. The chaff bombers performed an equally interesting and dangerous task. The aircraft assigned this mission were extremely vulnerable to MIG attack. Their external load decreased maneuverability and increased fuel consumption, and they had to fly straight and level to dispense their chaff. The chaffers were especially desirable targets because the North Vietnamese knew that SAMs were useless against strike aircraft flying in the chaff.

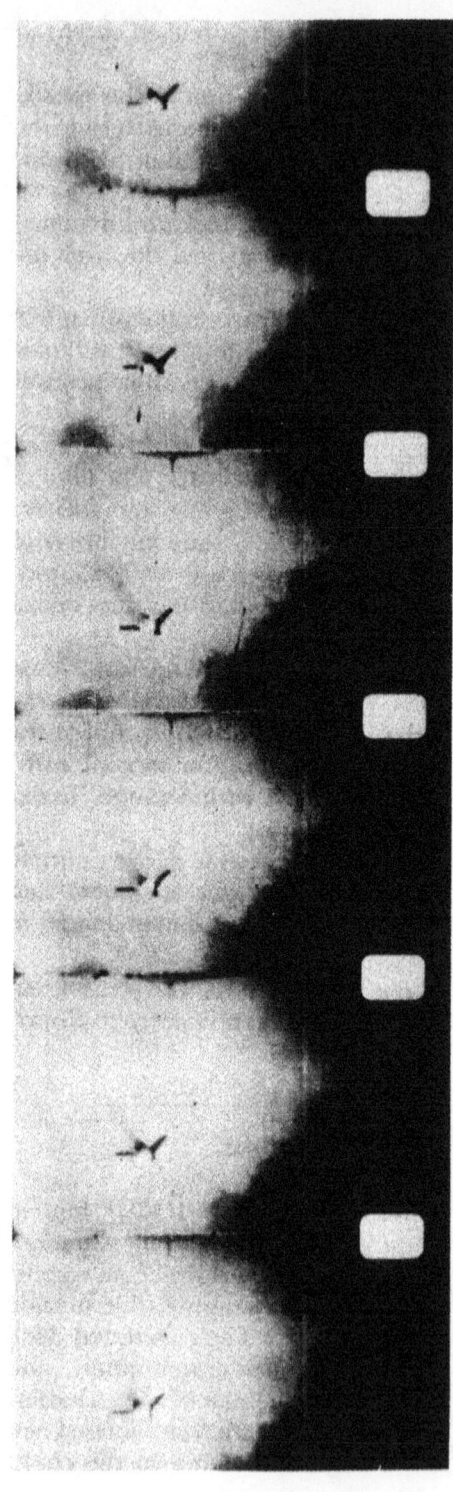

MIG-17 bursts into flames after being hit by 20mm cannon fire, 19 Sep 1966.

A pilot "suiting up" for a mission.

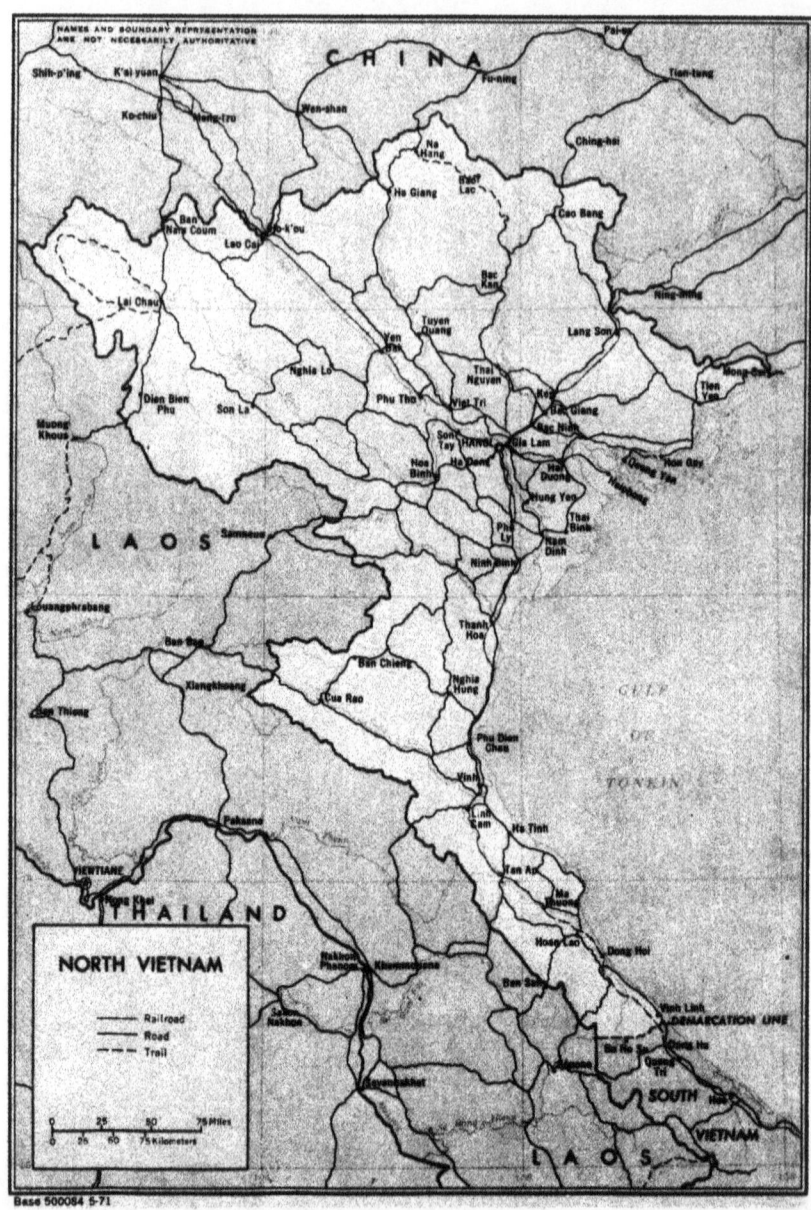

Also, chaff and escort aircraft airspeeds were slower and their posture much more defensive and reactive than that of the MIGCAP aircraft.

The chaff escort mission was equally hazardous and can be explained best by describing a typical Linebacker assignment. Finch, a flight of four F-4Es, was protecting Date flight, one of the two chaff flights operating on 12 September 1972. The primary target was the La Danh storage caves 35 miles north of Hanoi. Finch ingressed near the town of Hon Gay, on the east coast near Haiphong. The chaffers were about three miles ahead in line-abreast formation. Finch 1 and 2 were on the left flank, 3 and 4 on the right. Immediately, *Red Crown*, the Navy control destroyer, began issuing MIG advisories. As the force continued west-bound, MIGs scrambled and headed North to cross ahead of the strike force.

Finch 1, Lt Colonel Lyle L. Beckers, with WSO, First Lieutenant Thomas M. Griffin, interpreted the MIG warning properly and anticipated an attack on the chaff force form the right side. Finch 4 spotted the bandits at four o'clock high, in a right turn, at high speed.

Two MIG-21 bandits drove straight toward the chaffers in a pincher-type geometry attack. They disregarded the escorts, or failed to see them. Finch 3 and 4 engaged the MIG closest to them, with 1 and 2 slipping, apparently unobserved, into the other MIGs six o'clock position. Colonel Beckers' Sparrow missiles failed to launch as the MIG closed on the left hand chaff flight. At this point, Finch flight had called the chaffers into a break to the right, and both escort elements were hard on the heels of the NVN interpceptors.

Lyle Beckers stabbed his throttles into afterburner and reset switches to fire a Sidewinder heat-seeking missile. Just then the MIG launched a missile at the breaking chaffers. The missile narrowly missed Date 4 and impacted Date 3 in the aft section.

Date 3, crewed by Captain Rudolph W. Zuberbuhler and his WSO, Captain Fredrick C. McMurry, nursed their crippled fighter toward the Tonkin Gulf, hoping to get "feet wet" before ejecting. However, the bird became uncontrollable as they neared Phantom Ridge, north of Haiphong, and both ejected. They were subsequently taken prisoner, and were released on 29 March 1973.

Further complicating and confusing the air battle, a third MIG-21 flashed in, over-shooting Finch 1 and 2. Finch 2 had time to roll out of his turn and fire a Sidewinder at the fleeing MIG but was forced to roll back to stay with Lead prior to seeing the effects of his missile.

Consistent with typical hit and run tactics, as soon as the first MIG fired his missile, he dove toward the ground in a split-S maneuver. Beckers, with his wingman, followed the MIG down through this maneuver, and fired a Sidewinder which failed to guide. As the flight bottomed out and pulled up in a steep climb, Beckers fired a second Sidewinder which impacted the MIG's left wing without appearing to detonate. But the MIG's wing began to stream smoke and flames. Finch 1 decided to close in for a gun kill and moved in to about 1,000 feet. As he opened fire, Beckers noticed his tracers passing behind the MIG and eased the pipper ahead of the MIG until he could see hits all over the fuselage. Trailing smoke, the MIG fell off on a wing and impacted the ground.

Finch 3, flown by Major Gary Retterbush and backseater First

MIG being hit by 20mm cannon fire, 5 Jun 1967.

Lieutenant Daniel L. Autrey, also had difficulty with their radar missiles. After the initial attack, the MIG that Retterbush was pursuing disengaged without firing. Retterbush and Autrey turned into the MIG's six o'clock position and ripple-fired two missiles. The first failed to guide, and the second did not detonate. Gary then switched to his heat-seeking missiles and fired a Sidewinder that narrowly missed but caused the MIG to execute a Split "S." The MIG pilot eased his turn as he pulled out, allowing Gary to fire two more AIM-9s.

Both were near misses but failed to detonate. One went just under the MIG, the other over the canopy. Gary then switched to guns, began firing, and immediately hit the MIG's fuselage and left wing. Retterbush pressed the gun attack and saw bullets impacting the canopy area. In a few seconds, the MIG lost control, apparently stalled, and pitched downward in a wingover attitude. It disappeared from sight.

Fighter pilots in controlled training conditions seldom agree on the exact outcome of air combat engagements. Statistics are somewhat firmer if the combatants shoot real missiles and bullets. However, circumstances and characteristics of air battles still defy duplication after the smoke has cleared and pulses return to normal.

In this battle, uncertainty exists as to whether two or three MIGs were downed by Finch flight. Moreover, no one can be sure how many MIGs attacked Date chaff flight. Only a correlation with North Vietnamese statistics could determine how effective the Air Force was that day.

Reflections on Linebacker I

Much has been said and written on the fact that the military fought in Vietnam with one hand tied behind its back. It must not be forgotten, however, that the USAF is an arm of the national government which employs force as an instrument of national policy. That force, then, is governed in its degree of application by the policy of the US government in accordance with national objectives. Under these conditions, the rules of engagement became a "battlefield manifestation of national policy."

These were the rules under which airmen and other members of the armed forces fought; rules that limited and restricted the application of force. They served the political aspect of the war, yet reduced the military effectiveness of the force. The advent of Linebacker saw a reduction in political restraints, which, in turn, eased the rules of engagement and allowed strike forces to carry the war more effectively to the enemy. Airfields, hydro-electric plants, key bridges inside the Chinese buffer zone, and key military targets in and around Hanoi were removed from US political protection as the effort intensifed.

Operation Linebacker was considered a success by virtually all viewers. The primary elements contributing to this success were:

    1. The President's decisive action when the invasion began.
    2. The immediate response of airpower.
    3. The President's decision to allow the military to make target decisions, once general guidelines and rules were established.

4. The giant step forward in technology exemplified by the guided bombs and their pinpoint accuracy.

Within the mechanics of Linebacker itself, the outstanding contribution was in the defense suppression effort. By neutralizing and destroying the enemy early warning radar, AAA, SAM and MIG threat, the aircraft loss rate was kept at an acceptable level and the Linebacker strike force was able to operate effectively in any area of NVN. Thus, air superiority was achieved and sustained.

As the war progressed, the USAF tactics continually changed to meet new threats and to take advantage of increased capabilities provided by advances in technology. Significant in the evolution of air superiority tactics in Linebacker was: (1) the introduction of electronic capabilities that allowed missile shots without visual identification; (2) the activation of improved US warning and control of aircraft over NVN; (3) specialization of units and personnel, which made specific people and organizations experts in a given mission, thus greatly improving the counter-air capability; and (4) recognition of the need for an implementation of enhanced aerial combat training.

As the military objectives of Linebacker I were achieved, the political objectives for Linebacker were likewise deemed successful. As a consequence, bombing operations north of 20 degrees North were halted by the United States in October 1972 as a demonstration of US good faith. Negotiations toward a ceasefire, at the Paris peace talks, had led to apparent agreement in November, but hopes of reaching a final agreement were dashed by the intransigence of NVN. The stage was set for the final curtain, Operation Linebacker II.

Air-to-Air Losses to Date 30 November 1972

NVN
185
US 90

Chapter VI. Linebacker II and The End of Hostilities

Peace Negotiations

On 26 October 1972, the North Vietnamese announced they and the US had reached agreement on a nine-point peace plan. Dr. Kissinger agreed with the plan to withdraw all US forces from SVN in return for the release of US POWs within 60 days, but denied he had agreed to a NVN announced 31 October deadline for signing the accord. Nevertheless, he told the nation, ". . .we believe peace is at hand," and added that only a single three to four day negotiating session remained to work out final unresolved details.

Bombing of all except the southern part of NVN was immediately suspended. Significant difficulties remained, however, since South Vietnam's President Thieu publicly denounced the plan as a "surrender of the South Vietnamese people to the Communists."

Despite intense US public pressure to get prisoners of war home by Christmas, a final agreement could not be reached. One day after President Nixon was briefed by Dr. Kissinger on the latest stalemate, he gave the order, "Execute Linebacker II."

The Big Push

Operation Linebacker II called for the swift, massive application of airpower at the heart of NVN. This meant hitting Hanoi, Haiphong, and other key objectives vital to the North Vietnamese economy and national prestige. Political restraints were reduced. Targets that had been off limits in the past were added to the approved target list. Major military airfields, for example, had long been sanctuaries, yet they affected air superiority and were lucrative targets. The level of destructive power was substantially increased. Employment of the B-52 over Hanoi, for the first time, demonstrated the President's resolve to bring the war to an end as soon as possible. The B-52, with its 30-ton bombload, was many times larger in firepower than the fighter-bombers that had hit targets around the city in the past.

The immediate goals of this renewed bombing effort were twofold: one, to halt the massive communist resupply effort that gave Hanoi the capability to stage large-scale offensive operations in SVN, and two, to convince the North Vietnamese that a very early return to the negotiating table would be in their best interest.

Planning Considerations

The gravity of the situation was obvious. In the face of an already hostile public opinion, the President had elected to risk the loss of more aircraft and the capture of more American airmen. Every effort had to be made to keep losses to a minimum. However, during the restricted bombing, Hanoi had been undisturbed, once again, in its efforts to fortify and resupply antiaircraft artillery and missile sites. The sites constituted a formidable defense and were expected to take their toll of aircraft, particularly the B-52.

Despite the B-52's sophisticated electronic countermeasures capability, planners were concerned about the heavy concentration of surface-to-air missiles the bombers would face. Through a long process that compared experience with known offensive and defensive capabilities, experts estimated the US would lose three percent of the total force of fighters and bombers in the 12-day effort. This would be a costly price to pay, but not unacceptably high if it met the twofold goals of the new offensive.

Building a Strike Force

A successful penetration of defenses such as those found around Hanoi required the coordinated efforts of many specialists and a variety of aircraft. Most combat aircraft had the potential to complete a strike mission without assistance, but the loss rates of those trying to provide their own self-protection were unacceptably high. As Linebacker I and other previous operations against the North had illustrated, a force of specialized aircraft grouped for mutual protection stood a much better chance of both mission accomplishment and survival.

At the center of the strike force was the B-52. Because of their size and restricted maneuverability they were a lucrative target for both MIG interceptors and SAMs, and thus required a great deal of protection. Past efforts to neutralize the North Vietnamese defenses had to be magnified in order to assure accurate bomb delivery and to get the big birds safely home.

As stated earlier, chaff was an important strike force protection. By dispensing clouds of radar reflective tin foil ahead of the strike force, the fighters were able to obscure the bombers from searching SAM and GCI radar beams. But, the mission was dangerous for the dispensing aircraft. Chaff blossoming behind the releasing aircraft marked its position and made it a target for the SAM. The drag of the chaff dispensers combined with the flight profile robbed the chaff aircraft of their normal maneuverability. As a result, a number of aircraft were lost in this key role.

Bomber escort and combat air patrol missions were popular with the fighter pilots. The two missions differed in that escort flights accompanied the bombers, while the CAP flights roamed likely MIG activity areas. The objective was the same—stop MIG interceptors before they could reach the bomber force.

Tactics for countering air-to-air attacks changed dramatically before the Linebacker II campaign. The long range lock-on capability of the F-4 radar enhanced the ability of the escort and CAP flights to protect the strike force.

The F-105 Wild Weasel further protected the B-52s. Their reputation for destroying missile sites with anti-radiation missiles and general purpose bombs was well established. Overall, their anti-SAM tactics were quite effective in forcing the operators to resort to less accurate methods and tactics. EB-66s also gave mutual electronic countermeasures support to the powerful internal systems carried on each B-52.

Following its deployment to Thailand in September 1972, the F-111 was used to supplement the strike force capability. Using its terrain following radar, it was able to fly at low altitude, slip undetected into North Vietnam, and strike targets at night and in bad weather. Previously these conditions protected enemy targets against such accurate attacks. F-111s used their exceptional capabilities to deliver twelve 500-pound bombs on selected SAM sites and airfields just minutes before the main strike force arrived. Defenses were there by denied the preparation time they normally had while waiting for the bombers to arrive.

Finally, the task force included the many KC-135 tankers required to get the force to the target and back, and specialized rescue aircraft used to recover aircrews downed in enemy territory.

Overall, these new, more powerful strike forces were not unlike those used in Linebacker I. A change to night time strikes, employment of the F-111, and high altitude B-52 bombing were the most significant differences.

The First Three Days

Colonel Bill Brown, Vice Commander of U-Tapao's 307th Strategic Wing, had long awaited this moment. As an F-105 pilot on a

F–4 "Phantoms" on escort mission over North Vietnam.

EB-66 supported the B-52 with electronic countermeasure operations.

previous Vietnam tour, he had been able to hinder the enemy's war effort effectively, but never had he delivered such an awesome amount of firepower directly to the NVN heartland. On 18 December, the thunder of his exploding bombs announced the arrival of the first B-52 in the heavily defended Hanoi area.

In addition to targets in the immediate Hanoi area, the bombers also hit Kep and Hoa Lac Airfields located to the northeast and west respectively. B-52 tactics called for a southeast heading on the bomb run, with a steep turn of nearly 180 degrees immediately after bomb release.

Strong tail winds boosted the B-52's groundspeed to a comfortable 600 knots during the bomb runs, but caused most of the chaff to drift out of position. Thus, many of the bombers were not afforded this very valuable protection. Also, the advantage of a 100-knot tail wind to the target was quickly removed when it became a 100-knot head wind as the B-52s departed the target, thus extending their SAM-threat time.

The first cells of B-52s met stiff opposition as they made their bomb runs. Although heavy AAA reached the bombers' altitude it was unable to bring any of them down. Despite numerous firings throughout the 12-day effort, only one aircraft received AAA damage.

F-111 being prepared for a mission over NVN.

SAC B-52s releasing a string of 750-lb bombs.

MIGs also were quite active during the strikes and caused many aircrews great concern. Airman First Class Albert Moore, an 18-year-old B-52 tailgunner, had been calling out SAMs from his position in the Stratofortress. Suddenly, a strange blip on his radar screen announced a more immediate danger — MIG! As he watched a MIG-21 swing in behind and slightly left of the bomber, he called out a warning to the rest of the crew. There was little they could do since they were concentrating on the bomb release only seconds away. The MIG closed rapidly and dropped to a firing position behind the B-52. Airman Moore locked onto him with his radar and clamped down on the gun triggers. The B-52 shuddered as the four 50-caliber machine guns fired, and missed! Moore relaxed his grip a moment, then fired again, and missed! Airman Moore fired a third time as the MIG approached to within 1200 yards. After what seemed an eternity, the MIG's radar image suddenly ballooned and disappeared from his scope.

Technical Sergeant Larry Chute, a gunner on another B-52, saw the MIG on fire and falling away. He watched several pieces of the aircraft explode into a fireball and disappear in the undercast.

Albert Moore could not believe his eyes. The MIG was really gone. He had fired 800 rounds of ammunition and downed an enemy aircraft. His efforts earned him the Silver Star.

MIG-21 "Fishbed" over North Vietnam.

Airman Moore's encounter was subsequently recorded as one of two confirmed MIG kills by B-52 tailgunners. Although they posed a serious threat, MIGs were thwarted in their efforts to shoot down a B-52. The tailgunners, MIGCAP fighters, and bomber escort flights managed to hold them off despite repeated intercept attempts.

The most effective of Hanoi's defenses against the B-52 strike force was by far the surface-to-air missile. The SAMs were numerous, mobile, and accurate if not completely jammed.

By the time B-52 commander Lt Colonel Don Rissi of Collinsville, Illinois, led Charcoal, Ivory, and Ebony cells to the final turn point for their bombing runs on the Yen Vien railroad yard, nearly 50 SAMs had been fired at the strike force. One B-52 had been hit, but it returned to U-Tapao. Of the 17 SAMs fired at the last three cells in wave one, two hit Charcoal Lead. Rissi's "G" model B-52 was two minutes from bomb release when it received heavy crew compartment damage and began burning. The aircraft went out of control about 30 seconds later and the crew ejected. Charcoal 1 was the first B-52G lost to hostile fire, and only the second stratofortress downed by enemy action in over seven years of ARC LIGHT bombing operations. Only three of the six crewmen of Charcoal 1 were returned when the prisoners of war were repatriated. Colonel Rissi was not among them. Members of the crew confirmed that his injuries from the SAM had proved fatal.

Five hours later, Wave II met similar opposition from the SAMs. Another B-52G fell victim to SAMs in the target area shortly after releasing its bombs. Fortunately, the crew was able to bail out over friendly territory before the bomber exploded.

Wave III drew the heaviest opposition of the three attacks on the first day. Over 50 SAMs were fired at the B-52s in addition to heavy AAA fire and attempted intercepts by MIG-21s.

Nearly all the B-52 sorties were successful on the first day of Linebacker II operations despite the launching of over 200 SAMs at the force. However, three aircraft were lost and two others damaged by the missiles.

Planning on day two was similar; B-52s arrived in three waves, three-to-five hours apart, each wave of aircraft completing its bombing in about 30 minutes. F-111s again bombed airfields just prior to the bombers' arrival. Tactics were changed to keep the strike force in the chaff. Ingress and egress tracks remained generally the same. Two bombers were damaged by SAMs but none were lost despite more than 180 launchings.

Day three, 20 December, was generally a repeat of the force's tactics and timing used on the previous two days. One change called for the use of an additional ECM. Unfortunately, the similarity ended here as three B-52s were lost during the first of three strike waves. Two of the three losses in Wave I were "G" model B-52s, with older, unmodified ECM equipment on board. Wave II, with no bomber cells of unmodified "G" models, bombed its targets and suffered no SAM hits. However, three more bombers, two of them unmodified "G" models, from Wave III were destroyed. In three days, the toll of unmodified "G" losses stood at five. By contrast the modified "Gs" suffered only one damaged. Other B-52 models suffered the remaining losses.

Of the six B-52s lost on the third day, three were struck by SAMs before bomb release and three in the post-target turn. Debriefings indicated the North Vietnamese were allowing the first cells of each wave to pass while they plotted the approach routes and post-release turning points. They then salvoed SAMs into the subsequent cells' bomb release and post-target turn areas where the probability of hitting a B-52 was the greatest.

During the first three days of Linebacker II, drone photography indicated outstanding bombing results. However, there was little celebration as the SAMs were still very potent enemy weapons. Enemy counter-air tactics also were changing. For instance, MIGs would fly abreast the B-52s, measure their altitude and call the information to the SAM sites. Accurate salvoes of SAMs immediately after the MIGs departed indicated the information had been put to use.

Brigadier General Glenn R. Sullivan, Commander of the 17th Air Division, directed Colonel Brown, Vice Commander of the 307th Strategic Wing at U-Tapao, to chair a special tactics panel to review the situation and make recommendations. The panel recommended changes that included varying ingress and egress headings, crossing tracks between the initial point (IP) and the target, and introducing random altitudes and sudden altitude changes before the bomb release point and the post-target turn. It also recommended varying the time between bomb release and the post-target turn. Eighth Air Force authorized these changes beginning the fifth day of the operation.

The Tactics Change

Although the B-52s still flew a southeasterly bomb run heading on day four, several changes were made: waves were compressed to put all bombs on target in 15 minutes instead of 30; post-target turns were modified to allow an overwater exit from NVN; altitude separations were increased; and even more ECM equipment was used to jam the SAM radar.

Of the two aircraft lost to SAMs on day four, one apparently violated his cell integrity thus exposing itself to SAM radars. The second B-52 had simply run into an extremely heavy concentration of missiles.

On day five, 22 December, the tactics panel's rather sweeping proposals became effective. Using the new tactics the B-52 strike force devastated Haiphong's railroad yard and petroleum products storage area. No B-52 received damage.

As bomber tactics improved, MIGCAP tactics also became more effective. On 22 December, Lt Colonel Jim Brunson of Eddyville, Kentucky, was leading Buick flight, a four-ship flight of F-4Es out of Udorn RTAFB, to their assigned combat air patrol area, when they received a "bandit" call indicating MIGs were airborne near Hanoi. *Red Crown*, the primary intercept controller, acquired Buick flight as they entered NVN and immediately began giving Colonel Brunson vectors toward the MIGs.

Two MIG-21s were climbing through 29,000 feet altitude just west of Hanoi when *Red Crown* identified other friendly aircraft directly between Buick flight and the MIGs. When the bandits turned south, it became readily apparent they were also under radar control and strike force aircraft were their intended victims. Set up for a head-on intercept, Brunson locked-on with his radar and requested clearance to fire. Since friendly aircraft were still a factor, *Red Crown* insisted on a visual identification before granting clearance. Buick flight members jettisoned their external fuel tanks and accelerated.

Spotting the MIGs about 10,000 feet above him, Colonel Brunson led Buick flight in a steep climb while his WSO, Major Ralph Pickett, maintained a positive radar lock-on. With clearance to fire now granted, the steering dot centered, and a MIG-21 under his gunsight pipper, Brunson fired four radar guided missiles in rapid succession. The flight watched the missiles close for the kill. Guiding flawlessly, the first missile knocked the entire tail section off the lead MIG and sent it into an uncontrollable spin. Still in good formation, the flight turned to engage the second MIG, but it had accelerated and departed. With all aircraft low on fuel, Colonel Brunson led Buick flight back to base and one of the biggest celebrations of his career.

The Post-Christmas Operations

The Christmas day recess in Linebacker II operations apparently was used by the North Vietnamese to resupply the SAM sites. After a low of four missiles fired on 23 December and 14 fired on the 24th, 68 SAMs met the bombers on 26 December, the eighth day of massive strikes. Two aircraft were lost, one in the Hanoi area and one while attempting to land with battle damage at U-Tapao. Both were part of a strike force with restricted ECM protection.

The value of the new tactics was further demonstrated in the bombing of the Thai Nguyen railroad yard. Eighteen B-52s dropped their bombs and recovered unscathed even without the usual chaff protection. The chaff in this case had been laid over the heavily targeted Hanoi area.

Targeting for the Stratofortresses changed to include some of the troublesome SAM sites. In addition, nightly low-level raids by F-111 fighter-bombers now were divided between the airfields and SAM sites. Not unexpectedly, bombing the Sam sites gave the B-52s maximum exposure to the missiles. Moreover, at this very close range, radar burnthrough of ECM devices, allowing SAM operators to see through the jamming, was not altogether unlikely. One incident of a B-52 mission against a SAM site is as follows.

Captain John Mize of Shreveport, Louisiana, was on his fourth Linebacker II mission when 15 SAMs were fired at him as he released his bombs on a particularly active site. One SAM impacted the left wing of his B-52D as he executed a steep turn away from the target area. The tremendous concussion knocked out all four port engines and associated equipment. Shrapnel set one engine afire, and as red cockpit warning lights flashed, the airplane began to fall. Several thousand feet of altitude were lost before Captain Mize managed to get the big bird leveled off.

Nearly every system on the bomber was inoperative. There was no radar, ECM, or computers. Only one alternator, a radio, and the cockpit lights remained in operation. All instruments were out except the altimeter and airspeed indicator. Most of the six-man crew had received shrapnel injuries.

The B-52 was almost helpless because it no longer had the mutual protection of the other aircraft in the cell, and it had lost its self-protection equipment. The crew saw two more SAMs but they missed. Fortunately, no MIGs spotted the crippled aircraft.

After about ten minutes, the flaming engine burned itself out and the crew set about trying to nurse the aircraft back to friendly territory. Since the B-52 could not maintain altitude with only the four right wing engines operational, Captain Mize gradually descended to maintain flying airspeed. The navigators calculated that if the left wing held together, they could get to the Thailand border with only a small compromise of the 10,000 feet minimum recommended bailout altitude.

As they drew closer to the safety of Nakhon Phanom RTAFB, Thailand, the situation rapidly deteriorated. The bomb bay doors fell open, one landing gear started cycling up and down, and other electrical systems went astray. In spite of the crew's gallant efforts, it soon became obvious they would not be able to coax the rapidly descending bomber to a safe landing. Fortunately, when the bailout order was given, the B-52 was only eight miles from Nakhon Phanom. Each man ejected individually on Captain Mize's order. All ejection seats, except the navigator's which was damaged, functioned normally. When his failed, the navigator exited through the hole formed when the radar-navigator ejected. After assuring himself that everyone was safely out of the dying Superfortress, Captain Mize ejected. For his heroic efforts, he was awarded the Air Force Cross, the other crew members received the Distinquished Flying Cross. All crewmembers also received the Purple Heart.

The Final Thrust

Weather in the target area during Linebacker II compounded the problem of attacking enemy defenses. Throughout December, the dominant northeast monsoon brought almost daily low clouds to the NVN delta region. Broken to overcast conditions existed below 5000 feet altitude for most of the 12-day Linebacker II campaign. Weather clear enough to permit visual bombing existed less than 12 hours total during the entire period. This thwarted most efforts to use the deadly accurate laser guided bombs and emphasized the need for an all-weather tactical bombing capability.

By 28 December, however, the bombing and revised B-52 tactics had proven so effective that bombers were no longer lost or even damaged. Compression tactics allowed more than 100 bombers to release their bombs and depart within a 15-minute period. Varying altitudes and headings avoided the previously established flight patterns. Success was such that finding enough lucrative targets began to be a problem. MIG sorties dwindled and, as more SAM sites were struck, missile firings became sporadic and ineffective. Wave after wave of bombers pounded targets with relative impunity. The bombing could have proceeded indefinitley with little likelihood of further losses.

The following is arecount of the last USAF MIG kill in Southeast Asia; it occurred on 8 January 1973.

Crafty, a flight of two F-4s from the 4th Tactical Fighter Squadron, was assigned a night MIGCAP mission in support of B-52 strikes. They ingressed North Vietnam through the "Gorrilla's Head" and established their CAP about 70 miles southwest of Hanoi. The pilot of Crafty One was Captain Paul D. Howman. His backseater was First Lieutenant Lawrence W. Kullman. The following is Captain Howman's description of the kill.

> About five minutes after arriving on station, we were advised by *Red Crown* that a MIG was airborne out of Phuc Yen and was heading southwest toward the inbound strike force. They vectored us northwest and told us he had leveled at 13,000 feet. Passing through [a heading of] north, we picked him up on radar at about 60 miles. We were able to follow him most of the way in as the range decreased. At about 30 miles, I called 02 and we jettisoned our centerline tanks.

Crafty One and Two descended to 12,000 feet at 400 knots, still taking vectors. *Red Crown* turned them to a northeasterly heading. At 16 miles *Red Crown* cleared Crafty to fire. Captain Howman's account continues.

> At 10 miles I got a visual on an afterburner plume 20 degrees right and slightly high. I called him out to the backseater and put the pipper on him. At 6 miles Lt Kullman got a good full-system radar lock-on. Range was about 4 miles and overtake 900+ knots when I squeezed the trigger. The missile came off, did a little roll to the left, and tracked toward the "burner plume." It detonated about 50 feet short of his tail.
> I squeezed another one off at 2 miles range. This one just pulled some lead, then went straight for the MIG. It hit him in the fuselage and the airplane exploded and broke into three big flaming pieces.

After determining there were no more MIGs in the area, Crafty returned to orbit for their remaining CAP period. They returned to base without further incident.

This battle for the skies over North Vietnam was quite a contrast to the earliest battles. Now, in early January 1973, the air-to-air battle took on almost textbook form with negligible outside interference from either SAMs or AAA.

Air supremacy had been achieved!

The final air-to-air box score was:

NVN	193	aircraft lost
US	92	aircraft lost

Glossary

AAA	Anti-Aircraft Artillery
AW	Automatic Weapon
CBU	Cluster Bomb Unit
CINCPAC	Commander-in-Chief Pacific
DMZ	Demilitarized Zone
DRV	Democratic Republic of Vietnam
ECM	Electronic Counter Measures
EOGB	Electro-Optical Guided Bomb
EWO	Electronic Weapons Officer
GCI	Ground Control Intercept
HE	High Explosive
IP	Initial Point
JCS	Joint Chiefs of Staff
LGB	Laser Guided Bomb
LOC	Lines of Communication
MIA	Missing in Action
MIGCAP	Combat Air Patrol (for MIGs)
PACAF	Pacific Air Forces
POW	Prisoner of War
RESCAP	Combat Air Patrol (for Rescue Operations)
SAM	Surface to Air Missile
SEA	Southeast Asia
TOT	Time Over Target

Index

Aircraft
  A-1, 125
  A-7, 152-153
  B-52, 79, 175-179, 181, 183-186
  B-57, 12, 125
  C-130, 53, 55-56, 134
  CH-53, 153
  EB-66, 26, 53, 79, 88, 132, 177-178
  EC-121, 107, 128, 133-134
  F-4, 11, 16, 21-23, 76, 79, 88, 107, 110, 131, 133-134, 139, 142, 152, 154, 157-158, 178
  F-100, 12, 24, 31, 33, 114-115, 117, 120, 125, 133
  F-102, 113-114, 116, 120
  F-105, 11-15, 17-18, 31, 35, 37, 67, 75, 88, 115, 118, 125, 134
  F-111, 177, 180, 186
  KC-135, 15, 28-29, 31, 79, 84-85, 125, 153, 158, 177
  RF-4C, 140, 153
  RF-101, 27, 31-32, 124-125
Air Force Cross, 25, 187
air refueling, 28, 30
Anderson, Captain Ron, 129-130
Australian Air Force, 120-121
Autrey, First Lieutenant Daniel L., 172
ATOLL (missile), 107
Baily, Lt Colonel Griff, 109
Beckers, Lt Colonel Lyle L., 171
Benoit, Airman Johnny A., 55
BOLO, Operation, 139, 142-145
bombing halts, 63, 78
"BRIGHAM", 119
Brown, Colonel Bill, 177, 184
Brunson, Lt Colonel Jim, 185
Burbage, Major Paul, 104
Burdett, Colonel, 74
CAROLINA MOON, Operation, 52-53
Carrier Task Force 77, 44, 57
Case, Major Thomas F., 53-55
chaff, 84-85, 88, 107, 176-177
Chairsell, Colonel William S., 138
Chute, Technical Sergeant Larry, 182

Clanton, Captain Norman G., 54-55
Clarke, Captain Art, 129-130
Crews, Major Barton P., 149
Danang AB, RVN, 53-54, 115, 120
Debellevue, Captain Charles, 109, 159-160, 162
Democratic Republic of Vietnam (DRV), 1, 4, 40
Dien Bien Phu, 1
Doughty, Dan, 26
Eaves, Captain Stephen D., 159, 162
ECM, 26, 84, 135, 138-139, 145, 153, 157, 183-185
Edmondson, First Lieutenant "Rocky", 54-55
EOGB, 79, 85, 159
Feezel, First Lieutenant Tommy, 159, 162
Feinstein, Captain Jeff, 109
FREEDOM DAWN, Operation, 84
Gatef, Major Eli, 104
Gia Lam, 9, 112-113
Giap, General Vo Nguyen, 147
Giraudo, Colonel John, 68, 74
Griffin, Thomas M., 171
Gulf of Tonkin, 2, 112, 128
Haiphong Harbor, 6, 135, 146, 171, 185
Hall, George, 26
Hand, Lieutenant Bob, 22
Hanoi, 4-7, 78, 135, 146, 159-160, 173, 176, 183
Harris, Captain Carlyle S., 37-39, 69
Hicks, Terry, 26
Ho Chi Minh, 1, 9
Holcombe, Captain Ken, 129-130, 132
Hoffman, Major James, 104
Houchin, Colonel Laydd, 104-105
Howman, Captain Paul D., 187-188
"INVERT", 119
IRON HAND, 133, 137, 142, 154
Johnson, General Horold K., 3, 126
Johnson, Colonel Howard C., 145
Johnson, President Lyndon B., 2-4, 9, 63, 78, 125

191

Jones, Captain Keith W., Jr., 149
Kennedy, President John F., 12
Kissinger, Secretary Henry, 175
Korat AB, Thailand, 31, 34, 115
Kullman, First Lieutenant Lawrence W., 187-188
laser guided bomb (LGB), 79-83, 85, 89, 91, 150-152
"lessons learned", 120, 125
Levy, Lt Colonel Gene, 22
LINEBACKER I, 84-85, 88, 147, 149-150, 152, 156, 159, 173-174
LINEBACKER II, 103, 175, 177, 185-186
Locher, Captain Roger C., 147, 149, 159, 161-163, 165
Lodge, Major Robert A., 147, 149, 159, 161-163
Lotz, Major Blaine, 104
Lucas, Major Jon I., 166-167
Malloy, First Lieutenant Doug C., 166-167
Mao Tse Tung, 1
Marines (U.S.), 157
Markle, First Lieutenant John D., 159, 162-163
McCain, Admiral John S. J., 159
McClelland, Major William, 16, 20
McConnell, General John P., 3-4
McInerney, Lt Colonel James E., Jr., 25
McMurray, Captain Fred, 171
McNamara, Robert F., 4
Messet, Captain Mike, 88-90
Meyerholt, Captain Bill, 36
MIGCAP, 21, 24, 26, 88, 107, 120, 127, 139, 147, 156, 167
MIGS, 11, 16, 21, 26, 39, 50, 71, 76, 88, 103, 107-108, 110, 112-113, 122, 126-128, 130-131, 133-134, 139, 145-146, 161-162, 167, 171, 174, 182, 184-185
Miller, Colonel Carl S., 84
Mize, Captain John, 186-187
Momyer, General William W., 16, 67, 74
Monkey Mountain, 115
Moore, Airman First Class Albert, 182-183
Moore, Lt General Joe, 52-53, 131
National Liberation Front (NLF), 1
Navy (U.S.), 11, 21-23, 26, 28, 45-46, 56-57, 59, 62, 79, 86, 107, 135, 147, 151, 153, 157
Nelson, Lt Colonel Gordon F., 104-105
Nixon, Richard M., 78, 86, 147, 175

Ngo Dinh Diem, 1
NVN Air Force, 112-113
Olds, Colonel Robin, 74, 139, 141-144
organizations
  2nd Air Division, 52, 132
  4th TFS, 187
  7th Air Force, 16, 45, 67, 150
  8th TFW, 68-69, 71, 74, 83-84, 88, 92, 139
  17th Air Division, 184
  45th TFS, 128-129
  49th TFW, 148
  67th TFS, 31
  307th Strategic Wing, 177, 184
  333rd TFS, 141
  355th TFW, 68, 74-75
  388th TFW, 68, 74, 135, 138, 145
  432nd TRW, 152
  469th TFS, 74
  555th TFS, 152
  4252nd Strategic Wing, 28
PANAMA, 115
PEACOCK, 115
Pettit, Captain Lawrence, 159
Phuc Yen, 112-113, 145, 166, 187
Pickett, Major Ralph, 185
Piowaty, John, 74
Pitchford, Captain John, 24-25
Rawlins, Major Addison, 104
reconnaissance, 25, 45, 85
RED CROWN, 147, 149, 153, 160-161, 171, 185, 187-188
Remers, Major Richard T., 53-56
reprisal attacks, 3
Republic of Vietnam (RVN), 1
RESCAP, 28, 31, 38
Retterbush, Major Gary, 171-172
Richthofen, Baron Von, 108
Ritchie, Captain Steve, 107-110, 159-160, 162-163
Risner, Lt Colonel Robinson, 21-32, 34, 36-39
Rissi, Lt Colonel Don, 183
RIVIT TOP, 145
Roberts, Captain Tom, 129-130, 132
ROLLING THUNDER, 4, 12, 23, 31, 45, 67, 110, 124-125, 133-134, 145-146, 150
route packs, 44-45
Sams, Colonel M. S., 135
Schurr, Lt Colonel Harry W., 74
Shanahan, Joe, 26
Shannon, Captain Fred, 25, 74
Shields, Master Sergeant John R., 55
smart bomb, 57, 79

Smith, Captain Dave, 91
Stone, Captain John B., 144
Stavast, John, 26
Sullivan, Brigadier General Glenn R., 184
surface to air missile (SAM), 11, 23-24, 51, 56-57, 60, 71, 76, 103, 110, 122, 130, 131, 133-135, 145-146, 153, 167, 174, 183-185
Swarts, Major Barry, 104
Takhli AB, Thailand, 12, 34, 75, 115, 120
Theiu, President, 1-2, 175
Thud Ridge, $1, 160, 166
Tonkin Gulf Resolution, 3
Trier, Captain Bob, 24-25
Turner, Staff Sergeant Aubrey B., 55
Turner, First Lieutenant Thomas M., 55
Ubon AB, Thailand, 115
Udorn AB, Thailand, 115, 185
U Tapao AB, Thailand, 183-185
Venanzi, Gerry, 26
Viet Minh, 1, 9
Vogt, General John W., Jr., 150, 159
Walker, Major Ron, 105
Walleye, ix, 57, 59, 62
Weyand, General Fred C., 159
White, Colonel Bob, 68
Wild Weasel, 21, 24, 76, 133, 135, 157, 177
YANKEE STATION, 45-46
YOUNG TIGER, 28
Zuberbuhler, Captain Rudolph W., 105, 171

193

www.ingramcontent.com/pod-product-compliance
Lightning Source LLC
Chambersburg PA
CBHW030139170426
43199CB00008B/129